THE LAST VAMPIRE

'My grandfather was the last of the Draculas. I do change into a bat occasionally but I wouldn't *dream* of sucking anyone's blood. As a matter of fact, I'm a vegetarian. I'm simply mad about oranges.'

On a camping holiday somewhere in Europe the Hollins family encounter rather more than they had bargained for. They find themselves involved in a hilarious adventure – which takes them deep into vampireland.

The Last Vampire

WILLIS HALL

Illustrated by
Babette Cole

Fontana Young Lions

First published in Great Britain 1982
by The Bodley Head Ltd
First published in Fontana Lions 1984
by William Collins Sons & Co Ltd
8 Grafton Street, London W1
Second impression May 1984

Reproduced, printed and bound in Great Britain by
Hazell Watson & Viney Limited,
Member of the BPCC Group,
Aylesbury, Bucks

I

"It strikes me," said Albert Hollins, glancing over his shoulder
into the back of the car where his wife was sitting, "that you
don't even know what *country* we're in—let alone what road
we're on!"

Their slightly rusting, dust-covered family car, its boot and
luggage-rack both bulging with camping equipment, was
parked precariously on a narrow, twisting, bumpy road flanked
on one side by a sheer, mountainous drop and on the other by a
dark and gloomy pine-forest.

Emily Hollins, surrounded as she was by countless unfolded tourist-maps, open road-books and motoring-guides, did not attempt to contradict her husband. "It isn't easy," she countered, "knowing exactly where you are in Europe—it's not like being in England when you're driving on the Continent."

Mr Hollins shook his head in exasperation and glanced at their son, Henry, who was sitting next to him. "What *is* your mum talking about?" he said, and added: "Can you understand her? Because I'm blowed if I can!"

Henry, who had no wish to take sides, shrugged noncommittally.

"What I'm saying is, that when you're driving around Europe you can cross so many borders and frontiers it's difficult to pinpoint your exact position," said Emily. She broke off to return the unblinking gaze of a passing mountain-goat which, chewing methodically, had paused to look at her through the rear window. It was not until she had stared out the mountain-goat and it had ambled on its way that Emily continued: "When you're driving around England you *know* you're in England—until you drive into the sea."

Albert Hollins sighed and puffed out his cheeks. "Surely you must have *some* idea where we are, Emily?" he said. "Belgium? Austria? Germany? France?"

Emily Hollins circled her forefinger over a large map of Europe, closed her eyes, and prepared to make a jab at it. "Eeny-meeny-miny-mo. . ." she began.

"That's no good at all!" wailed Albert. "I don't even know what we're doing here! Why did we have to come? Why couldn't we have gone, as per usual, to the Sea View Hotel at good old Cockleton-on-Sea? We never, ever get lost there—all we have to do is cross over the promenade from the hotel to the beach. Right, Henry?"

Henry shuffled in his seat and gave another non-committal grunt.

"It's all your fault, Emily," continued Albert. "I knew we were in for trouble from the very moment you brought those travel brochures into the house! That's when our troubles first began!"

It had all started one muggy, overcast afternoon when Emily Hollins had been on her way home from her weekly trip to the supermarket. A quick cloudburst had sent her scurrying for shelter, a plastic bag of groceries bouncing in each hand, into a nearby travel agent's shop. Once inside, and rather than stand gazing bleakly at the rain drumming on the window, she had turned her attention to the row upon row of colourful brochures that were there simply for the taking.

Two Glorious Weeks in the Sunny Algarve!
Fifteen Exciting Days in New York and Miami!
Luxurious Self-catering Villas in Barbados!
Sun-drenched Beaches on the Bay of Naples!
Spectacular Coach-trips through the Austrian Tyrol!

And there and then, as she flipped through the pages, a magical new world had opened up for Emily Hollins.

As the rain outside in the High Street had eased off to a mere constant drizzle, Emily had snatched up as many of the brochures as she could cram into her already overloaded shopping-bags and carried them home.

For weeks Emily had spent every single moment of her spare time poring over the brochures. Over her morning coffee, she had toyed with the idea of luxuriating on a palm-fringed beach. As she had nibbled at her weekday boiled-egg lunch, she had daydreamed about Waldorf Salads served up beside swimming-pools in Californian grand hotels. And, as she had sat up in bed, while Albert pleaded with her to switch off the bedroom light, she had spent more precious moments going through brochures until, finally, she dropped off to sleep and dreamt of lounging back in a first-class cabin on a night-flight bound for Torremolinos.

Emily's dedication paid off at last. As the April showers died away and May arrived—bringing with it still more showers—a joint decision was arrived at by the Hollins family. This year, it was agreed, instead of their usual holiday at Cockleton-on-Sea, they would spread their wings and go abroad!

And not *just* a holiday abroad: a camping holiday! Fifteen full days during which they would not be tied down to any one hotel but would be able to travel freely, wheresoever the fancy took them, sampling the delights of Europe.

"Haven't you got *any* idea at all of where we are, Emily?" demanded Albert for the umpteenth time, as the car stuttered and coughed its way uphill.

Emily thought hard. "Germany," she said at last.

"Are you *sure*?"

There was a long pause. "Almost sure. I think we turned right and right again in Belgium—round that pretty little market-place where we bought those onions."

"They weren't onions—it was garlic," growled Albert, with bitter memories and the faint after-taste of a cheese-and-garlic sarnie that Emily had concocted for him two nights before.

"They *looked* like onions," said Emily. "How was I to know? Anyway, I think it was there that we went wrong—we should have turned left and left again for France, but we turned right and right again instead. I'm almost certain we *are* in Germany, Albert, now that I come to think of it."

"Oh?" said Albert. "And what's brought you to that opinion?"

"Do you remember that last border check-point we came through? The one with the barbed wire and the dear little sentry-hut with the roses growing up the side?"

"No," said Albert, shaking his head, slowly.

"Yes, you *do*! Of course you do! You remember it, don't you, Henry? The one with the guard who shouted a lot when your father was showing him our passports?"

"Oh, yes!" said Albert, before Henry had time to answer. "I do remember him. The one who went red in the face and waved his arms about a lot. I don't think he'd have let us through either, if I hadn't been too quick for him and put my foot down on the accelerator."

"I'm positive he was German," said Emily.

"What makes you think so?"

"It was the things he said."

"But you don't understand German," said the puzzled Albert.

"No," said Emily. "But he *sounded* German. And, in any case, he had a German moustache."

Albert Hollins sighed, shook his head despairingly and

turned to his son. "I *knew* we should have gone to Cockleton-on-Sea," he said. "Life would have been *so* much easier: a paddle in the ocean, a snooze in a deckchair, back to the Sea View for a roast and three veg. Instead of which, here we are, somewhere in Europe, stuck up a mountain with your mother as guide and map-reader. And what do we discover? That she's been planning our route by the shape of men's moustaches! I give up! Where do *you* think we are?"

Henry scrubbed at the dust-caked window with the heel of his clenched fist, but the grime was all on the outside. He wound down the window and peered out.

The scenery had hardly changed at all since the last time Henry had examined it. The sheer mountain-face still fell away, breathtaking but dangerous, on one side of the car while, on the other, the dark and brooding pine-forest bordered the winding road for as far as the eye could see, silent and seemingly impenetrable.

"I don't know where we are either, Dad," announced Henry. "But it certainly *looks* more like Germany than France."

Albert Hollins swung hard at the steering-wheel in order to negotiate an awkward bend. The bumpy mountain road, he realized, was getting steeper and more narrow. What was more, now that the car window was open, Albert felt he could detect a dampness in the air that suggested mist. The sun, too, was dipping towards a distant mountain-top and evening could not be all that far away.

"We'll have to find a field or a farm or somewhere soon to stick the tent up," muttered Albert.

"A cup of tea, that's what I'm looking forward to," said Emily.

"Keep your eyes skinned, both of you, for a turning off this road," said Albert.

"We just passed one," said Emily.

"What?"

"A turning. A road going off through that forest."

"I never saw it. Did you, Henry?"

"No, Dad."

"*I* saw it," said Emily, firmly. "Definitely. It wasn't much of a road, mind you. But it was wide enough to drive along."

Albert Hollins threw his wife a suspicious glance over his shoulder but, all the same, he put the gear-lever into reverse and backed, slowly and carefully, down the mountain road.

Emily had been right. There *was* a turning off into the forest. And it was hardly surprising that neither Albert nor Henry had noticed it. You couldn't really call it a road, more of an overgrown cart-track and almost covered with fallen pine-needles. The thick pine-branches formed a dark canopy over the track through which no light had penetrated for many years; pitch darkness lay ahead of them in the forest.

Albert switched on the car's headlights and eased it forward, gently, off the mountain road towards the gap between the tall trees.

"There are some gate-posts," said Henry.

"Where?" asked Albert.

"There." Henry pointed just inside the perimeter of the forest.

Albert braked the car and looked where Henry had pointed.

He could see them now in the glare of the headlights: a pair of moss-and-ivy-covered dark grey stone gate-posts, reaching up, some twelve or thirteen feet, into the lower branches of the

pine-trees. There was a kind of crumbling statue on top of the
left-hand post. It had once been some sinister sort of bird,
thought Albert, sitting on top of a stone ball with its wings
outstretched—although both of the wings had long since fallen
off or worn away. He could just make out the remnants of
another stone ball on the right-hand gate-post where, he imagined, a similar carved bird had also once perched. There
must have been heavy wrought-iron gates between the posts in
some long-forgotten day but these had rusted off or been carted
away for scrap many years before. Albert eased the car forward,
gently, between the crumbling gate-posts and then it picked up
speed, crunching into the thick carpet of pine-needles that
covered the track.

The beam from the headlights stabbed into the trees that lined the track ahead of them but, on either side of the car, the darkness was close and oppressively gloomy. They had left the evening sunlight far behind and there was no sign of daylight ahead. Quite the reverse in fact, for the deeper they drove into the forest, the darker and more sinister it became. The track, which they had taken in the belief that it would lead them straight through and out the quickest way the other side, was proving to have a mind of its own, and twisted and turned and even, on occasion, doubled back on itself. There was nothing for it but to press on, even though the narrow track was getting twistier and bumpier and, like the forest itself, seemed to go on for ever.

Nothing like this ever happened at Cockleton-on-Sea, Albert told himself. In fact, on their yearly holiday at Cockleton-on-Sea there was never any need to get behind a steering-wheel at all—except for when he went on the Dodgem-cars on the pier! Next year, Albert told himself, would be different. He would put his foot down. Travel brochures or no travel brochures. Next year would find them back at the good old reliable, tried and tested, Sea View Hotel! Albert smiled with anticipatory pleasure.

Emily was also silent. Camping holidays were all very well in their own way, she said to herself, but she felt she had allowed herself to be talked too easily into this one. Next year she would put her foot down and they would take their holiday at a proper hotel. And not the dreary Sea View place neither! No, Emily knew *exactly* where she intended to stay next year. She had sat and studied it so many times that now the travel brochure fell open automatically at the right page. It was an enormous holiday hotel on the Spanish Riviera. There were eight hundred bedrooms, each one of which had its own bathroom and sun-trap balcony; there were two swimming pools, three dining-rooms *and* a snack-bar which was open in high season. There was a colour photograph in the travel brochure which showed the happy occupants of the eight hundred rooms enjoying themselves on the golden sun-drenched beach with the giant hotel in the background, painted pink and white and looking for all the world like an enormous, mouth-watering, birthday cake! Emily allowed herself a secret smile in anticipation of the next year's treat that was in store.

Henry Hollins was silent too. But the thoughts racing round in his mind had nothing to do with next year's holidays. Henry was far too concerned with what was going on, at that moment, in his immediate surroundings.

He was staring, mouth agape, through the open car window into the depths of the forest where, glowing brightly in the darkness, he could make out two pairs of eyes staring unblink-

ingly back at him. Then, as his own eyes became accustomed to staring into the darkness, he began to see more eyes, all of them unmoving and all of them gazing steadily back at him. And all just too tantalizingly far away from the car for him to make out who they belonged to. They were too far from the ground for any of the smaller creatures of the woodland such as rabbits or squirrels or even foxes. On the other hand, they were not high enough for human beings. Unless, of course, they belonged to very *small* human beings? *Pygmies?* Of course not! There weren't any pygmies on the Continent. What about woodland dwarfs? Even more ridiculous! No, Henry was quite sure that the eyes belonged to some kind of animal or other. All right then—what kind of animals stood almost a metre high whose habitat was European forests? One answer flashed immediately into Henry's head. *Wolves!* Henry gulped.

Surely not? The idea was too unlikely to be spoken aloud. For one thing, he didn't want to frighten his mother—for another, his father would surely laugh at him.

Henry kept his thought to himself but, just to be on the safe side, he wound up the car window as tightly as he could.

The car cruised on, deeper and deeper into the ever-thickening forest.

2

"Are you quite *sure* you didn't see anything of a wooden mallet when we packed up this morning?" said Albert, pulling hard at one of the guy-ropes on the tent, holding a tent-peg in his other hand and looking around for something with which to bang it into the ground.

Emily shook her head. "I know I didn't touch it, Albert," she said. "What I'm short of," she continued, scrabbling in the boot of the car, "is that little twisty-wire-thing that fits on top of the stove—the one the kettle sits on—I don't suppose you remember seeing that on your travels?"

Albert shook his head, firmly. "Are you all right for a minute, Henry?" he called.

"Yes, Dad!" Henry's muffled voice came back from underneath the hanging folds of the half-erected tent where he was holding up, temporarily, one of the main tent-poles.

Albert Hollins crawled around on his hands and knees looking for the missing mallet, while Emily dug deeper and deeper into the boot of the car in search of the "twisty-wire-thing" without which the kettle would not rest on top of the stove.

The Hollins family were pitching camp.

The rambling track along which they had driven through the

forest had emerged, quite suddenly and to all their delights, out of the trees and into the open of a late-evening orange sunset. Albert had stopped the car and they had clambered out to find themselves on a grassy slope which stretched ahead to where the grass gave way to a jagged cliff-face towering above them, half in shadow in the fading light.

And so, with the car parked by the edge of the forest, they were now trying to get the tent up and the kettle boiling before they were overtaken by the night.

"Found it!" cried Emily, emerging in triumph from the boot of the car and holding aloft the "twisty-wire-thing". "Soon have the kettle boiling now!" she added, and then her smile turned into a frown. "Albert Hollins! Whatever do you think you're doing?" said Emily.

Albert, who was busily thumping a tent-peg into the ground, glanced up. "What's the matter, Emily?" he asked.

"I hope you know that's my best kettle you're using for a hammer!"

"Sorry, Emily," said Albert, glancing at the kettle in his hand and giving his wife an apologetic smile. "I couldn't find the mallet anywhere—I wonder what's become of it?"

"You'll be wondering what's become of your bed-time cocoa too," said Emily, "when you've dented my kettle so that I can't boil any water up!"

"I'm afraid we'll all have to go without our bed-time drinks tonight, Emily," said Albert. "A kettle's not much use without something to put in it—and there's no time left tonight to go looking round for a stream or spring. It'll be dark before we know where we are."

"I wasn't thinking of looking for water anywhere," said Emily.

"Oh? And how did you imagine you were going to fill the kettle then? Wave a blinking magic wand, I suppose!"

"No," said Emily, coldly. "I was going to ask someone."

Albert threw back his head and laughed. "*Ask* someone?" He extended both his arms, taking in all of their surroundings: the darkening forest on one side, the looming mountain-face on another and, stretching away beyond them into the shadowy horizon, the desolate scrubland. "*Ask* someone!" he repeated. "We're at the back of the beyond, Emily! There's not a soul for miles! I shouldn't think anyone's been anywhere *near* here since the year dot! Who the blue blazes do you think you're going to ask?"

Emily sniffed and pointed, calmly, towards the foot of the mountain. "I was going to try that castle there," she said.

Albert followed her glance and blinked, twice. His eyebrows shot up. His mouth dropped open in surprise. For there, nestling in the lower, rocky slopes of the mountain was a gaunt, grey castle which, he was willing to swear, had not been there five minutes before.

"Well, I'll be jiggered!" said Albert. "Where did that place spring from?"

"It's *always* been there," said Emily. "For hundreds of years and more, I shouldn't wonder."

"How come I didn't notice it before, then?" said Albert.

"Because you were probably too busy crawling around on your hands and knees looking for your mallet," said Emily.

Albert pretended not to hear this and stood gazing at the castle. He rubbed his chin. It was an unfriendly-looking sort of place, he decided. There were odd turrets that jutted out at peculiar angles and lots of small towers with red-tiled pointed roofs. The grey stone walls were dotted, higgledy piggledy, with small arched mullioned windows that seemed to peer out, black and forbidding, in the eerie orange glow of the setting sun.

"I wonder who lives there?" said Albert.

"There's only one sure way to find out," said Emily, firmly. "Pass me that kettle!"

"Supposing we're trespassing on private land?"

"Oh, go on with you!" said Emily, briskly. "We're not doing any damage. *I'm* not afraid to go round to the back door of that castle and ask them to fill the kettle with water. You can stay here and finish putting the tent up."

Albert turned his attention away from the castle. He pointed, proudly, at the tent which, although he didn't seem to notice, was leaning over at an awkward angle. "It is up!" he said. "And in double-quick time too!"

"Should it be leaning over quite like that?" said Emily.

"It *isn't* leaning over!" snapped Albert. "I should know. I had years and years of training in the Boy Scouts. That's a perfect example of how to pitch a tent!"

To add weight to his words, Albert raised the kettle in the air and brought it down on the last tent-peg with a resounding *thwack*!

The tent-peg trembled under the blow and then slid, slowly but ever so surely, out of the ground and, once free, shot up in the air. The over-taut guy-rope snapped back on the tent canvas, putting an extra burden on the next tent-peg which, in turn, was dragged out of the earth.

Albert watched helplessly as, one by one, all round the tent, like a row of collapsing dominoes, the tent-pegs were tugged out of their moorings and leapt in the air. Then the tent canvas, supported only by the main poles, teetered for several seconds before it collapsed in an untidy heap on top of Henry.

"Well done, Albert!" said Emily. "Was it your years of Boy Scout training that made it come down like that?"

"There's no need to be sarcastic," snapped Albert. "It's all right, son!" he called, and: "Keep still! We'll soon have you out!"

Albert Hollins was as good as his word. Moments later, Henry was standing beside his parents gazing down at the heap of canvas.

Emily shook her head, clucked her teeth and snatched the

dented kettle out of Albert's hand. "I'll take this," she said, "before you do any more damage!" She proffered the kettle to Henry and pointed up the slope. "Do you fancy a walk up as far as that castle, Henry, while I give your father a hand with that tent? Go round to the back door and ask them, very nicely, if they'd oblige us with a filling of water."

Henry's eyes widened in mild surprise. Like his father, he had been unaware of the castle's presence until his mother pointed it out to him.

He set off, swinging the battered kettle in his hand and leaping from one clump of thick grass to the next, up the slope towards the curious, ancient building at the foot of the mountain. Before long, the grass gave way to loose shingle and then Henry felt beneath his feet a firm, uneven surface. He glanced down and discovered that he had struck a cobbled path which led up to the front of the castle. Looking along the path in the opposite direction, although it was overgrown with grass and weeds, he could see that it went into the forest. It occurred to him that he was walking along what had once been a driveway and that it probably joined up with the pine-needle-carpeted track they had taken through the forest. The crumbling gate-posts through which they had entered the forest must once have marked the boundary of the castle's grounds.

In times gone by, thought Henry, shining horse-drawn carriages must have rattled along that self-same driveway, carrying dukes and duchesses and other grand personages with their ladies all in their finery, to grand occasions at the castle: balls and banquets, feasts and celebrations. Gallant noblemen, in gleaming uniforms and polished boots, on prancing snow-white chargers had, no doubt, galloped off to war along the driveway through the forest—and some of them had ridden back, in glory, and others had never ridden through the forest again. . .

He stopped. He looked up. Without noticing, while lost in his thoughts, he had arrived outside the castle which, as the sun dipped down behind the rim of the mountain, was bathed in shadow.

Henry shivered. A chill breeze had whipped up from somewhere and, inside the castle walls, an unfastened door or window-shutter was banging to and fro. There was no other sound from within and he had a feeling that the place was empty. It had a cold and lonely deserted air. Surely, if anyone had been living in the castle he would have been aware of some sort of presence by now?

Continuing along the cobbled driveway, he made his way towards a pair of huge wooden gates which, he guessed, would open on to the castle's courtyard. The ancient iron-studded gates were firmly locked but a small door, let into one of the gates, groaned slightly at his touch. He pushed harder. The rusted hinges squealed complainingly, but the small door creaked open. He stuck his head through and peered around.

"Hello?" he said, nervously. "Anyone at home?"

There was no sound save for that of the breeze as it rustled, uneasily, through a pile of fallen leaves in a corner of the courtyard.

"Hello?" he called again, but louder than before.

"Hello-o-o-o . . . !" The cry came drifting back at him.

Henry gulped, swallowed hard, and then relaxed a little as he realized there was an echo in the courtyard.

"Is anyone there!"

" . . . anyone there-ere-ere-ere. . .!"

The unfastened door or window-shutter rattled again somewhere and several dried leaves took off from the pile and
scuttled across the grey-green flagstones.

Silence again.

Henry turned, slowly, and studied the inner walls. There
was nothing but blackness behind the cobwebby windows. All
the doors were firmly locked and barred.

He had just made up his mind to set off back to the camp-site
when he spotted the old cast-iron pump in a corner of the
courtyard. Commonsense told him that there would be little
point in seeing if it worked. In all probability, he told himself,
the pump had stood there idle for years and years. But having
come this far, he decided he was not going to go back empty-
handed, not without pursuing every avenue. He strode across,
quickly, to the corner where the pump stood.

Something caught his eye. There was a stone with a carved inscription on it set into the courtyard wall, close to the pump and just above his head. In order to read the words he had to stand on tiptoe and peer closely at the worn stone. He could just make out the thick, large letters:

THE
CASTLE
ALUCARD

And, above the words, there was carved the same strange birdlike figure with outstretched wings that he had seen on top of the crumbling gate-posts at the other side of the forest. His previous assumption had been correct, then? Those gate-posts *had* originally marked the entrance to the castle grounds.

Turning his attention to the pump, Henry pushed the top of the kettle underneath the spout and tugged the pump-handle, expecting it to be stiff and rusty. But, surprisingly, the pump worked smoothly at his touch. Two pulls at the handle and a jet of clear, crystal water shot out of the spout and, in no time at all, the kettle was brimming full and he was running out of the courtyard and down the grassy slope.

Albert meanwhile, with Emily's able assistance, had succeeded in putting up the tent—a trifle lopsidedly, it was true, but, Albert insisted, that was because they had pitched it on a slope.

Before long, they had boiled the kettle on the stove and the three of them were lying snug in their sleeping-bags, Emily and Albert in one of the tent's compartments and Henry in the other, with mugs of cocoa at their elbows.

Emily, by the light of the lamp, was having a last flick through a couple of the travel brochures she had brought along with her on the trip.

Albert watched her, disapprovingly. He removed a sliver of milky skin from the top of his cocoa daintily with his little finger, and shook his head. "I've heard of some things in my time," he said, "but I've never heard of anyone who spent their holiday reading holiday brochures!"

Emily ignored him. Tucked up in her thoughts, Emily was miles away on a palm-fringed, sun-kissed Hawaiian beach, sipping at an ice-cool coconut drink and allowing the smooth warm sand to trickle between her toes.

Albert, getting no response from Emily, turned his attention to Henry. "I hope this water you brought is safe to drink!" he called through the canvas tent-divider. "Pump-water sounds a bit dicey to me—we could all end up with dodgy tummies! Are you sure you knocked hard enough on that castle door?"

"There wasn't any need to knock, Dad!" Henry called back. "It's deserted—nobody lives there!"

"It wouldn't have done any harm to knock," Albert muttered to himself, "just to be sure—" He paused, frowned, put his head on one side, and listened carefully for several moments; then, "Can you hear anything, Emily?" he said.

Emily, who had moved on from the Hawaiian beach to a first-class cabin on a fortnight's cruise in the Mediterranean, looked up in irritation at Albert's intrusion. "Hear what?" she said. "All I can hear is you, interrupting my thoughts!"

Albert shook his head, pettishly. "No! Listen!" he said. "I'm sure I heard some sort of music!"

"*Music?*" Emily stared at her husband as if he had gone out of his mind. "Music?" she said again. "In this outlandish place?"

"Listen!" Albert held up a silencing forefinger. "Listen, Emily! There it is again!"

Emily cocked an ear and listened, hard. "Goodness me!" she said. Albert was right. He *had* heard distant music. And now Emily could hear it too. Softly, and some distance away: the sad song of a violin, rising and falling on the wind. "Well, would you believe it!" she said, astonished.

Albert scrambled, in his pyjamas, out of his sleeping-bag and tugged at the strings on the tent-doors. Henry, who had also heard the sound, joined him. Albert's fumbling fingers managed, at last, to untie the knots on the tent-door strings. Together with his son, he stared out into the night.

The moon had risen, casting a pale light over the entire countryside. The tops of the pine-trees were silvery fronds, swaying in the wind. The castle too was bathed in a pale glow, its turrets and towers standing in ghostly silhouette against the tall, black mountainside.

The moon slipped behind a passing cloud, shrouding the castle in darkness.

Albert stared, hard. He thought he could see a small circle of yellowish light shining out through one of the arched windows. He rubbed his eyes and looked again. Yes, definitely! A tiny, flickering glow such as might come from an oil-lamp, or possibly only a candle. Was that, he wondered, where the music had come from too?

"I said you should have knocked hard on the castle door," he observed to Henry.

"What do you mean?"

"Can't you see that light in the window?"

Henry shook his head. "What light?" he asked. "Which window? Where?"

"*That* window—there!" said Albert, pointing at where the glow had come from.

But the moon had come out again, lighting up the castle walls, and the tiny glow was no longer visible. The music seemed to have stopped too—either that or the wind that carried the sound to the tent had changed direction.

"I can't see anything, Dad," said Henry.

Albert decided it was something that could wait until the morning. "Never mind," he said. "It doesn't matter now. Let's go back to bed."

Emily tucked her travel brochures underneath her pillow, for safety, as her husband snuggled back inside his sleeping-bag. "What was all that about, Albert?" she asked. "Did you find out where that violin music was coming from?"

"I've a jolly good idea," he replied. "I *said* there was somebody living inside that castle." He leaned across and turned down the lamp.

There were several moments of silence and then Emily heard her husband struggling to sit up again.

"Whatever is the matter now?" she said.

"Didn't you hear that?"

"Don't tell me you've been hearing music again?"

"No! Dogs barking. That *proves* the castle's inhabited."

"I can't hear anything."

"*Listen!*"

"*Ah-whoooOOOOO! . . . Ah-whoooOOOOO!*"

The cry drifted across, clearly, on the night air.

"Oooh, yes!" said Emily, also sitting up in her sleeping-bag. "Now I can hear them!"

"Vicious brutes they sound as well!" said Albert. "*Just* like the Hound of the Baskervilles! It wouldn't surprise me in the least if they're let loose on us tomorrow. Trespassing on private ground, without so much as an excuse-me or a by-your-leave!" Albert raised his voice and called to his son through the canvas tent-divider. "Can you hear those dogs, Henry? Perhaps now you'll believe there's someone living inside the castle!"

Henry did not reply. He was thinking, hard. The moon was peering in at him through a gap in the tent-flap. He pulled the sleeping-bag up around his ears, curled up tight and chewed, nervously, at his lower lip. Several things were worrying him and he tried to put them in order.

Firstly, the howling that he could hear didn't sound, to him, as if it was being made by dogs. Secondly, it didn't sound as if it was coming from the direction of the castle either. He listened again.

"*Ah-whoooOOOOO! . . . Ah-WhoooOOOOO!*"

It sounded, to Henry, as if it was coming from the pine-trees.

And, if it *was* coming from the pine-trees, and if it *wasn't* dogs . . . His first suspicions must have been right—there was a dangerous pack of howling wolves wandering in the forest!

There was another matter, too, that was worrying Henry. He had been puzzling for some time about the carved inscription he had seen, inside the courtyard, on the castle wall:

THE

CASTLE ALUCARD

There was something strange about that name. It had just occurred to him what it was. He shivered and snuggled down, deeper, inside his sleeping-bag.

ALUCARD spelled DRACULA backwards.

3

Things looked better, as they are often inclined to do, in the warm glow of morning.

The sun had risen early, bathing the mountain-top in a rosy hue and spilling its golden fingers across the countryside. The pine-forest presented an altogether cheerier picture in a brighter shade of green. The slope on which the Hollins family had pitched the tent seemed more like an early autumnal meadow than the grim wasteland it had seemed in the grey mist of the previous evening. And even the Castle Alucard had lost its cold forbidding appearance of the night before.

Emily Hollins was frying sausages and tomatoes and Albert rubbed his hands together briskly, delighted at the prospect of the breakfast to come. "I say! Those sausages do look good!" And then he turned and smiled at Henry who was coming out of the tent. "Well, young man, and what's on your agenda for this morning? Anything in particular planned?"

"No, Dad." Henry's eyebrows shot up, questioningly. "Why? Aren't we packing up and moving on after breakfast?"

Albert smiled and shook his head.

"I thought you thought we were trespassing?" said Emily.

"It did cross my mind last night, yes," said Albert. He

glanced across towards the castle and then continued: "But I think if anyone up there had any objections to our being here they'd have let us know by now. No, I think we could go much further and fare far worse than this place."

Emily looked doubtful. "It's a bit out of the way, Albert, isn't it? I mean, it isn't like being on a *proper* camp-site."

"True, true," said Albert. "On the other hand, that's something in its favour. I mean, do you know how much they *charged* us at that site in Belgium the other night? They must have seen us coming! An absolute rip-off that place was! And, I ask you, what had it got to offer that this place hasn't?"

"Hot and cold water," said Henry.

"We've got *cold* water here," replied Albert, "and plenty of it—in that pump you found."

"But that belongs to the castle," said Henry.

"Yes, yes—but they don't seem to mind us using it. And if we want some *hot* water we can always boil a kettle up. What else are we short of?"

Emily looked down at the ground, shuffled her feet awkwardly, and raised a delicate subject. "Well," she said, "it hasn't got a you-know-what, has it?"

"What's a you-know-what?"

"You *know*," said Emily, blushing. "A place to spend a penny."

"Oh! One of *those*! No, I'll grant you that it doesn't come with all mod. cons. But it won't do us any harm to rough it for a day or two." He glanced across towards the edge of the forest. "And if we are caught short," he added, "we can always pop into the trees."

Henry blinked. It was his duty, he thought, to tell his

parents about the roaming pack of wolves. But if he did so, he felt sure they would only laugh at him. He decided to hold his tongue. But there were also his fears regarding the castle and he wondered if he should voice those. He decided to take a chance. "That castle . . ." he began.

"What about it?" said Albert.

"There's an inscription on the courtyard wall."

"Oh, yes?"

"It's called the Castle Alucard."

"Is it, indeed?" said Albert. "I'll bet it's been there for a year or two. We must take some snaps of it before we go. We'll get some with us standing in front of it."

Henry took a deep breath and then plunged on: "Alucard," he said, "is Dracula spelt backwards."

"Really?" said Albert, disinterestedly. "That's a coincidence."

"Breakfast's ready!" said Emily.

Henry sighed, shrugged to himself, and sat down on the folding canvas chair that his mother had set out for him at the folding camp-table. He had done his best. He had tried to warn them. It was no good. Oh, well. . .

He tucked into the heaped plate of sausages and tomatoes that had been put in front of him.

Albert Hollins hummed to himself as he steered the car out through the crumbling gate-posts at the edge of the pine-forest and set off, driving carefully, up the winding mountain road. He had left his wife and son behind to their own devices at the camp-site, to go off foraging on his own.

Not that he was pleasure-bent. Far from it. For one thing, he intended to find out where they were. Because of Emily's dismal failure as map-reader on the holiday, they didn't know for certain which country they were in. Emily had plumped for Germany, but she could easily be wrong. France, perhaps? Or they could have been driving round in circles and be back in Belgium?

It was a very unsatisfactory situation. After all, what kind of a silly ass was he going to look when he got back home and was showing his holiday snaps to Trevor and Enid Perkins, their next-door neighbours? He could just imagine the scene! "Yes, Trevor, this is a photograph of Emily and me standing in front of a French *château*—or else a German *Schloss*." And, in his mind's eye, he could see Mr Perkins nudging Mrs Perkins and saying in that know-all voice of his: "Get a little lost, did you, Albert, old lad? We thought you might be overdoing it rather when you said you were motoring round the Continent!" No, that wouldn't do at all! It was important that he pinpoint their position exactly!

There was also the question of provisions. There were plenty of tinned food-stuffs back at the camp-site, but they needed fresh vegetables, bread, milk, eggs, cheese—that kind of thing. If he could find a hamlet or a village then there would be a village shop. And, surely, the winding road must lead to one or the other? All roads, after all, led somewhere—otherwise they wouldn't be there. *All roads lead to Rome!* Now, who'd said that? Not that he imagined for one moment they'd arrived in Italy! Although, with Emily as navigator, you could never be sure of anything!

Albert smiled to himself as he swung the wheel, negotiating yet another tricky bend and then—lo and behold!—his problems were answered. There were signs of civilization up ahead.

He spotted a church-steeple first, jutting over the brow of a hill. Next he passed a whitewashed cottage in a field, and then a pair of cottages, and then a whole row of cottages. The winding road, he discovered, went right through the heart of a busy mountain village.

Pulling off the road, he parked the car in the cobbled market square. Albert switched off the engine and sat examining his surroundings. He studied the buildings bordering the square, looking for a clue as to his whereabouts. But the shops and houses gave nothing away. They were all half-timbered, whitewashed, quaint little buildings that didn't look particularly German *or* French—on the other hand, he decided, they could have been either!

Albert turned his attention to the villagers as they went about their business, either on foot or by horse and cart. But there was nothing to be gained from them. They looked like—well —like *villagers*! The women were wearing dirndl skirts and embroidered blouses and most of them had shawls over their heads. The menfolk were dressed in sleeveless sheepskin jackets and corduroy trousers and had neckerchiefs knotted at their throats.

There was only one thing for it, Albert told himself. He would have to get out of the car and make a personal approach.

Crossing the cobbled square, he approached an old man who was sitting on a bench sucking at an empty pipe.

"*Bonjour!*" said Albert, using the only word of French he knew.

The old man took his pipe out of his mouth, spat, and put his pipe back in again, but gave no sign that he had understood.

Ah-ha! Albert decided that he was getting somewhere. He had established that he was not in France.

Moving on, he strolled up to where an old woman was sitting in a doorway, plucking the feathers from a dead goose which she was holding between her knees.

He smiled at the old woman, cheerfully. *"Guten tag!"* said Albert, thus exhausting his entire command of the German language.

The old woman gazed back at him, stony-faced.

Oh-ho! Better still! Now he knew that he was not in Germany either. Where did that leave? Belgium? But wasn't the Belgian language the same as French? In that case, where on earth could he be? Denmark? Sweden? Norway? *Russia?* Anywhere on the blessed globe, I suppose, thought Albert, gloomily. And it was all Emily's fault.

He had made some slight progress though, he told himself. He was pretty sure that he wasn't in Holland because he hadn't seen anyone wearing clogs.

It was then that he noticed the little general shop with the low door, standing at one corner of the village square. The shop's window was full of long, thin, cooked sausages hanging on strings and all sizes and shapes of cheeses.

A small, brass bell jangled above the shop door as Albert pushed it open and walked inside. The shop, which was dark and full of nooks and crannies, smelled of herbs, spices, paraffin and scrubbed wood.

Another door behind the high, black counter creaked open and the shopkeeper appeared. He was a bald-headed man with a spotless apron tied around his paunch. He looked Albert up and down, wiped his hands on a dishcloth and beamed,

genially. "Good morning, sir!" he said.

"Good heavens!" said Albert. "You speak English?"

"Oh, yes, sir," said the shopkeeper. "We have visitors from all over the world passing through the village. Either on their way up the mountain, or on their way down. It's useful, in my job, to speak a language or two. I can usually tell, too, where folk are from just by looking at them."

"Is that a fact?" said Albert. He glanced around the shop, every inch of which seemed to be packed from floor to ceiling with all manner of goods. He would certainly be able to buy everything he needed here.

"And in which direction are you heading, sir?" said the shopkeeper. "Up the mountain or down?"

"Neither," said Albert. "As a matter of fact, I'm thinking of stopping over in the district for a day or two." He paused and pointed at a large round red cheese that took his fancy. "Do you think I might have half a kilo of that?" he asked.

"Of course, sir," said the shopkeeper, placing the cheese on a board and picking up a long, sharp knife. "Stopping over, eh? Looking for lodgings, are you?" The shopkeeper shook his head as he slid the knife through the cheese. "You might have a little difficulty there, sir. There's no hotel in the village and folk round here don't look too kindly on taking strangers into their homes—they like to lock their doors at night and keep themselves to themselves."

"No, no, no," said Albert. "I'm not looking for accommodation. I'm here on a camping holiday with my wife, Emily, and my son. We've got a tent. *And* we've found an ideal spot to set up camp."

"Have you indeed, sir?" said the shopkeeper, slapping the slice of cheese on to a sheet of greaseproof paper and weighing it on an old-fashioned cast-iron pair of scales. "And where might that be?"

"Just down the road a mile or so and through a forest. We've found a quite delightful secluded spot. We've pitched our tent by the Castle Alucard. Do you happen to know the place by any—"

Albert broke off in some surprise as the shopkeeper's knife dropped from his grasp and clattered, noisily, on to the flagstone floor. The man made no attempt to pick it up. His hands were shaking and his eyes had opened wide. He backed away from the counter, fearfully.

"Is anything the matter?" said Albert.

The shopkeeper made no reply but turned and scuttled through the door behind the counter. There was the sound of a key turning in a rusty lock and then there was silence.

Albert waited, patiently, for several minutes. He whistled soundlessly between his teeth and outlined patterns on the flagstones with the toe of his shoe. Then, glancing at his watch, he took a coin from his pocket and rapped it on the counter. "Hello?" he called, and: "Anyone there? I'd like to pay for this cheese and there are one or two other things I'd like to purchase!"

Absolute silence.

He glanced towards the door through which the shopkeeper had made his hasty exit. There was no way in which Albert could be certain of the fact, but he had the distinct impression that an eye was peering at him through the keyhole. Deciding that he was not staying there to be made a fool of, he turned and walked out, briskly.

The brass bell jangled above Albert's head as the shop door slammed shut behind him.

Albert Hollins sat in the driving-seat of his parked car and pondered on his lack of success. He had not bought any groceries. He had not discovered where he was. He remained there for some time, gazing, morosely, across the cobbled square, and wondered what to do next.

Across the square, the old man still sucked on his empty pipe as the old woman sat in her doorway, plucking away, in a cloud of goose-down.

Emily Hollins tapped the top of the corned beef can and the slab of meat slid out, effortlessly, on to the bright red plastic plate.

> *"Country-living's*
> *A way of giving*
> *Everyone a smile*
> *Every country mile. . ."*

Emily trilled to herself, happily, as she went about her chores. This was the part of the day that she enjoyed the most on their camping holiday: the time when she was left alone to get on with things.

Albert had gone off in the car to buy some groceries and find out where they were. Henry, having helped with washing up the breakfast things, had gone off, as boys are wont to do on holiday, to explore their surroundings and, no doubt, dirty his knees and tear his pullover, bless him!

Emily Hollins had tidied the tent, shaken the sleeping-bags and hung them out to air. She was now preparing a stew for lunch. It was a recipe she had concocted herself from what was to hand and would contain: tinned corned beef, tinned potatoes, tinned carrots, tinned beans and tinned peas. There would also be tinned peaches and tinned cream to follow.

She smiled to herself as she diced the corned beef into small squares. As soon as the stew was ready for the stove, she thought, she would allow herself fifteen minutes off for a hot drink and a flick through a couple of travel brochures.

The idea of a Winter Break had been nagging away at the back of her mind for some days now, and she wanted to get some firm plans into her head before broaching the possibility with Albert. What was it to be? A couple of weeks skiing down the crisp, white slopes at Kitzbuhel? Or a fifteen-day package holiday sampling the winter sun on the Atlantic coast at a posh Miami hotel? It was a difficult decision and, while she was pondering over it, she got the curious feeling that she was not alone.

Emily glanced up. She was right. A huge Alsatian dog, the biggest she had ever seen, was standing no more than a few yards away from where she was working, growling at her menacingly.

Emily stared at the wolf—for wolf it was, although she didn't realize it.

The wolf stared back at Emily.

"Good doggie!" said Emily.

In reply, the wolf splayed its front feet, lowered its head, drew back its upper lip and showed her an ugly set of gleaming teeth.

"GgggggrrrRRRR!" snarled the wolf, undecided only as to which part of Emily it should sink its fangs into first.

"*Naughty* dog," said Emily.

"GgggggggRRRRRRRRRR!" went the wolf again, louder than before. The grey-brown fur rose all along its back. Its jaws were twitching. Saliva dripped from its heavy jowls.

"*GGGGGGGGRRRRRRRRRRRRRR!*"

"*Bad* boy!" said Emily. As a child she had owned a poodle and so she had grown up with no fear of dogs at all. "Who's a *naughty, naughty* dog den? Who's a *bad, bad* boy for growling at Auntie Emily?"

The wolf was somewhat taken aback. It had not had much previous experience of humans in the forest but the few that it had come face to face with had either taken refuge up a tree or disappeared over the horizon at a nifty rate of miles per hour. It would allow this person one last chance, the wolf decided, to do a disappearing act, failing which it would take a mouthful of Emily's plump calf.

The wolf threw back its head and let out a terrifying howl. "*AH-WHOOOOOOOOWLLLL!*"

It occurred to Emily, at last, what was the matter with the animal. "Aw, diddums den!" she said, sympathetically. "Is the lickle doggie-woggie hungry? Does the lickle doggie-woggie's cruel master at the castle not give him enough to eat?" With which, she picked up one of the cubes of corned beef and held it, temptingly, above her head.

The wolf cocked its head on one side and sniffed. All food was food, it decided. The wolf put aside, temporarily, all thought of taking a mouthful out of Emily's leg and concentrated its attention on the succulent morsel that the human was holding in the air. The wolf took two paces towards Emily and opened wide its jaws.

"Catch, boy!" Emily tossed the cube of corned beef towards the wolf which caught it, neatly, and swallowed it at a gulp.

Mmmmmm! The wolf licked its lips. Really good. Delicious, in fact! The wolf couldn't remember when it had tasted quite so tasty a snack before!

Life in the forest, these days, was not all that good. Over the last few years, the wolf-pack had increased in numbers and the demand for food had outgrown supply. Whenever a piece of fresh meat, such as a rabbit or a hare, did become available, it had to be shared out with all the wolf's companions—and, given the opportunity, the wolf-pack could devour a rabbit in seconds like a . . . well, like a pack of wolves. In any case, the wolf wasn't all that fond of rabbit. Tiny bits of fur tended to get stuck between its teeth and the small bones stuck at the back of its throat. . .

"Here, boy! Good boy!" Emily held up another cube of corned beef. "Who's a clever dog, then!"

The wolf could hardly believe its good fortune! It took the second cube as neatly as it had caught the first and swallowed it in an instant.

Emily "tut-tutted" and shook her head. The poor thing

didn't look as if it had enjoyed a good meal in years! They probably starved their watch dogs up at the castle. Just look at the mangy state of its fur! *And* she could count its ribs! Had she been home, she would have reported the castle-owner to the R.S.P.C.A. But foreigners, as she well knew, didn't show the same respect for their pets as people did in England. Luckily, they had brought with them on the trip a plentiful supply of canned meats. She would, she resolved, give the entire contents of the tin of corned beef to the dog.

It proved to be the finest and tastiest meal that the wolf had had in years. One tin of corned beef might not have seemed much to a healthy Alsatian dog, but to a half-starved wolf, who had been known to exist for a week on a single stringy rabbit-leg, the corned beef was an entire feast.

"Good dog! Good boy!" said Emily, as the wolf sniffed at the ground and licked up the last crumbs of meat that had fallen from its mouth. Emily crossed from behind the table and held out her hand to stroke the wolf. "Who's a good boy, then? Who's a clever man?" she said, encouragingly.

The wolf sniffed at Emily's thumb. It wondered, for a second or two, whether the hand that was being stretched out towards it was intended as some sort of second course? But, luckily for Emily, it quickly rejected the idea. Wolves are crafty creatures. It had never heard of the expression: "never bite the hand that feeds you". But some sort of simple animal philosophy of a similar nature went through its mind.

All the same, the wolf had *some* natural pride and dignity. It certainly wasn't going to stand around while the strange fearless person prodded at it. The wolf turned and slunk off, the way it had come, into the shelter of the pine-forest.

What a nice dog, thought Emily. And how well-behaved too. It was a pity that the people at the castle didn't know how to treat their pets properly.

Sighing to herself at the stupidity of foreigners, she took herself into the tent in search of another can of meat to put into the stew.

Sergeant Alphonse Kropotel peered out of the iron-barred window of the police-station, across the cobbled square, to where the stranger was sitting at the wheel of the parked car. The sergeant narrowed his eyes, tugged at his tunic, and turned back into the office. He looked at the man who was standing on the other side of the desk and who was rubbing his hands, nervously, on the spotless apron that was tied round his paunch.

"You're *sure* that's what he said, Eric?" demanded the sergeant.

The shopkeeper, whose name was Eric Horowitz, nodded, firmly. "Definitely, Sergeant! The Castle Alucard, he said! I heard him with my own ears!"

Sergeant Kropotel stroked his beard and sucked in his cheeks. "The Castle Alucard?" he said. "But why would anyone in their right mind go anywhere near that place? Even to

45

get there would mean travelling through the forest . . . think of the wolves, Eric!"

The shopkeeper shuddered. "I often *do* think of the wolves," he said. "*Too* often! Sometimes I try *not* to think of them, but it's no good. I lie in bed at night and listen to them howling fiendishly in that forest. It's the same with my wife."

Kropotel's eyebrows shot up in surprise. "Why, Eric? Does your Irma howl fiendishly at night too?"

"No, no, no," said the shopkeeper, impatiently. "I mean she can't sleep either for the wolves!"

"Ah!" The police-sergeant shrugged and spread his hands, palms upward, expressively. "Tell me anyone in this village that can?" he said. "And, as if the wolves weren't bad enough, there's also. . ." He broke off, as if the thing that he was about to name was too awful a word to be said aloud.

The shopkeeper nodded, nervously. "Of course," he said, "there's also. . ." and he, too, found it impossible to complete the sentence.

"If I had had my way," continued Kropotel, "that dreadful castle, and all it stands for, would have been burned to the ground years ago—yes, and the forest as well!"

"It's no good saying now what *should* have been done," said the shopkeeper. "The fact of the matter is that the Castle Alucard is still standing. What's more to the point," he paused and jerked his head towards the village square, "is what does that stranger want with the place?"

"Does he travel alone?" asked the police-sergeant.

The shopkeeper shook his head. "He's got his family with him—or so he says. His wife and son."

"Three of them?" said the police-sergeant, apprehensively.

46

"Yes! Three of them! At the Castle Alucard! And what are they doing there, I'd like to know? And what do you propose to do about it?"

"Nothing."

"Nothing?"

"What can I do?"

"Your job! What you are paid to do! Arrest him, of course!"

"What for?" Kropotel fiddled with a pair of ancient handcuffs which were on his desk. "We don't know for certain that he is a v-v-v-v-v. . ." and again the policeman's voice broke off, and then continued: " . . . and even if he is, we've got no proof."

"*Proof?* What kind of proof do you *need*? I suppose you're going to sit around, doing nothing, till we all wake up one morning dead in our beds!" snorted the shopkeeper.

"Not at all," replied Kropotel. "I shall commence my enquiries immediately. And also, you may be sure, I shall keep a watchful eye on the fellow." In order to add weight to his words, Sergeant Kropotel turned and stared, hard, through the barred window, across the cobbled square at the subject of their conversation.

Albert Hollins, sitting in his parked car, shuffled uneasily in his seat. He had the definite feeling that he was being watched. Funny? That was the second time it had happened since he had arrived in the village. First in the shop, when he'd been sure that someone was spying on him through the keyhole—and now here.

Turning his head, cautiously, he glanced around the square. Yes! There was a pair of eyes staring over at him from behind a barred window! I've had enough of this, thought Albert.

47

Switching on the engine, he released the brakes and drove off the cobbled square, back on to the narrow road by which he had come.

A moment later, Sergeant Kropotel strode out of the police-station, adjusting the hat-strap under his chin. He was carrying a swagger-stick which he tapped, thoughtfully, against his highly polished knee-length boot as he watched the car pulling off down the road. He was ready to begin his enquiries. Gazing around the square he noticed an old man sitting on a bench, sucking at an empty pipe, and an old woman sitting in a doorway in a cloud of goose-feathers.

The old man on the bench looked up as Sergeant Kropotel approached him.

"Good morning, Ernst," said Kropotel.

The old man took the pipe out of his mouth and spat on the cobblestones. "Good morning, Sergeant," he said.

Kropotel pointed along the road in the direction that the car had taken. "The stranger who was in that car?"

"Yes?"

"I don't suppose you happened to notice anything special about him?"

The old man took off his hat, scratched at his wrinkled bald head, spat again, and shrugged. "Only that he was French."

"*French?*" Sergeant Kropotel frowned.

"Yes."

"But Horowitz, the shopkeeper, was sure that he was English."

The old man shook his head and peered inside the empty bowl of his pipe. "Horowitz is a fool. The man was French without a shadow of doubt."

"Are you sure of that?"

"He said '*Bonjour*' to me," growled the old man. "What more proof do you want than that?"

Sergeant Kropotel's brow was furrowed in thought as he crossed to where the old woman sat in the doorway. The plucked goose was lying beside her. She now held the carcase of a duck between her knees.

"Good morning, Elsa," said Kropotel.

The old woman's gnarled fingers fluttered ceaselessly over the duck's body and feathers flew everywhere. "Good-day to you, Sergeant Kropotel," she muttered, toothlessly.

The police-sergeant pointed across the cobbled square with his swagger-stick. "The stranger who was sitting in the car not long ago," he said.

"What about him?"

"I was wondering if you happened to notice anything special about him?"

The old woman removed a feather which had got lodged somehow in her hair, and shrugged. "Only that he was German," she said.

"*German?*" Kropotel could hardly believe his ears. "Are you *sure?*"

"Of course I'm sure. He said '*Guten tag*' to me. What more proof do you want than that?"

Sergeant Kropotel shook his head, mystified, and walked away. He tapped his cane against the side of his boot in familiar fashion—a sure sign that he was deep in thought.

So? The stranger had pretended to be three different things to three different villagers? *Why?* For what possible reason? And which of the three nationalities that he had adopted had been his real one? English? French? German? One thing was certain though. The stranger had something to hide. Without doubt, he was up to no good. Well, whatever foul deed the stranger had in mind, Kropotel would foil his evil plans.

It had been many years now since the last lot of trouble in the village. Sergeant Kropotel shivered at the ghostly memories of the past. It was up to him, Police-Sergeant Alphonse Kropotel, to make sure that the horrors of an age gone by remained dead and buried for all time.

Kropotel drew himself up to his full height, pulled in his chin, stuck out his chest, and strode across the cobbled square towards the police-station. There was work to be done. He would begin by questioning every single one of the villagers.

Albert Hollins had not driven very far. He had parked his car on the winding road opposite the pair of whitewashed cottages on the outskirts of the village. He was sitting in the driving-seat, looking at an apple-cheeked countrywoman who was throwing corn to her chickens.

Albert was still unhappy at the thought of returning to the camp-site and having to admit to Emily that his trip had been entirely unsuccessful. There was still a slight chance that he might discover their exact geographical location. He had failed in the market-place with his attempts at German and French but another opportunity had suddenly presented itself.

Albert got out of the car and walked towards the garden-fence smiling and waving, cheerfully, at the countrywoman. He had just remembered how to say "Good morning!" in Italian.

4

Henry Hollins set off to walk round the Castle Alucard for the fourth time that morning. Deep in his trouser pocket his hand trembled, slightly, as it kept a tight hold on the garlic bulb.

Vampires, he knew, were afraid of garlic. It was lucky that his mother had not put all of the garlic bulbs that she had bought in the Belgian market-place into the cheese sandwiches she had made for his father. Henry was sure that there was a vampire hiding, somewhere, inside the castle. Who else had been playing the violin the night before? Who else had lit the oil-lamp, or candle, that his father was sure he had seen? Certainly no ordinary human being, for the castle courtyard had proved as empty and deserted in the morning sunlight as it had seemed in the lengthening shadows of the previous evening. All of the doors and windows were shut tight, which was why he was now walking round and round the castle walls in search of some other means of entry.

It *had* been Dracula's castle once, he was sure of that. As well as his discovery about the name spelt backwards, there were also the carved figures on the crumbling gates repeated on the courtyard wall. He now realized that they were not birds, as he had thought at first, but bats. Vampire-bats. It *had* to be a vampire's castle. For this reason, he had gone back to the camp-site to arm himself with the garlic bulb.

Emily, as usual, had got her nose stuck in a travel brochure and had failed to notice her son's return. Henry had taken what he had come for out of the vegetable box and now, holding it tightly in his clenched fist, was exploring the outside of the castle walls.

A sudden flutter and rush of wings, coming from almost underneath his feet, caused him to stand stockstill with fright and sent his heart leaping, or so it seemed, into his mouth.

But the beating wings belonged, he realized, to nothing more sinister than a game-bird, sitting on a clutch of eggs, whose nest he had almost trodden on. Henry let out a long sigh of relief as he watched the bird gain height and sweep across the country-side and then he too continued on his way.

Apart from those in the courtyard, there were no doors to be seen on the outside of the castle. The great, thick walls rose up to where the towers and the turrets jutted out above his head. Even the lowest of the windows were too high for him to reach and, if they *had* been within his grasp, he told himself, they were far too small for him to squeeze his body through.

He was never going to find a way in, he decided. As soon as he had completed his circuit of the castle, he would give up the search and go back down the slopes to play in the quarry or by the stream. But no sooner had he taken the decision to abandon his quest when he spotted something he hadn't seen before.

"Where did that come from?" he asked himself. It was a narrow flight of worn stone steps leading down the side of the back wall of the castle, below ground level, to a small dark iron-studded door.

There was a blackened iron ring for a door-handle which, he discovered, was rusted into place and his attempts at turning it with one hand proved fruitless. Henry was forced to relinquish his grip on the garlic bulb in his pocket in order to use both hands to turn the iron ring.

The latch grated and then the door creaked open, slowly.

A wave of cold, damp, stale-smelling air struck him square in the face as he stepped inside. He was in some sort of cellar. It was a large, empty, vaulted room that stretched away, as far as he could make out, into sinister-looking shadowy corners.

"Hello?" he called, taking a nervous step across the uneven

stone-flagged floor. There was no reply. "And answer came there none," he muttered to himself, but couldn't think where the quotation came from. He took another tentative step into the room.

The door through which he had entered swung shut behind him of its own accord, plunging the cellar into darkness. Henry was about to retrace his footsteps when, peering ahead, he made out another flight of stone steps, going up this time. At the very top there was a thin streak of daylight coming from underneath a door which must, he realized, lead into one of the ground-floor rooms. His feet clattered up the stone steps. He found himself standing in a long, high-ceilinged, stone-walled dining-hall which, it seemed, had not been used for many a long year. Tattered, faded banners hung from a minstrels' gallery. There was a long refectory dining-table down the centre of the hall on which there stood two silver candlesticks hung with cobwebs. The padded seats of the twenty or so dining-chairs that surrounded the table were decorated with exquisite brocade and the chair-backs were finely carved, each one embellished with the letter D.

"D for Dracula!" he murmured to himself and he felt the hair prickle along the back of his neck and the blood tingling in his veins.

Then, glancing up, he thought he caught a glimpse of movement on the minstrels' gallery. He couldn't be sure what it was—just a flash of scarlet and black as someone or some*thing* darted through an archway.

"Hey! Stop!" called Henry. "Wait a minute—you up there!"

But once again there was silence, except for the faint scuttling of a mouse or a rat in the hall's huge fireplace.

There was an opening in one corner of the hall inside which was a spiral stone staircase that looked as if it led up to the gallery. Henry sprinted across the dining-hall and took the stone steps two at a time. The spiral steps *did* take him up to the gallery and the archway led him up another flight of spiral steps, narrower this time, and at the top of these he found himself in a circular stone room.

"That's funny!" he said to himself. For there was no one in the room. He was willing to swear that whoever—or *what*ever —he'd seen from downstairs had come up here. There was no other exit apart from a tiny arched window which was much too small for anyone to climb through. Henry frowned and then, dismissing the vexing puzzle from his mind, turned to look at his surroundings.

The circular room was filled with antique, though comfortable, furniture and looked oddly like a large Victorian bed-sitting-room. There was a big armchair by the fireplace, an upright chair, a table, a chest-of-drawers and a large wardrobe. What was more, the room had obviously been in recent use. There was a candlestick on the table containing a candle that was half burned through, and there were fresh ashes in the fireplace giving evidence of a fire on the previous night. Henry also discovered a smaller table, half hidden from his sight by the large armchair, on which there stood an old-fashioned wind-up gramophone with an enormous horn and a record already on the turntable.

Henry, out of curiosity, wound up the gramophone and, as the turntable picked up speed, lifted the needle-arm and placed it in the record groove.

The sad song of a violin crackled out of the giant horn.

So his father *had* heard music the night before! And it had come from this room! And that candle must have provided the light that his father had said he had seen! But who or what or, indeed, *where* was the mysterious person or thing that had been responsible for playing the gramophone? It was the same person, Henry felt sure, that he had caught a glimpse of on the minstrels' gallery.

The gramophone-needle stuck in a crack in the old record and the same mournful notes were repeated, again and again, from the horn.

Henry switched off the gramophone. He had, he decided, done sufficient exploring for the time being. He was just about to leave the room when he noticed the piece of scarlet-lined black cloth that was wedged in the wardrobe door.

Someone was hiding in the wardrobe!

Henry gulped, twice. What should he do next? Now that he was almost face to face with the mysterious person, Henry felt a twinge of fear. Should he stand his ground, open the wardrobe door, and confront whoever was in there? Or tiptoe quietly from the room and report back to the camp-site?

It was a difficult decision. It was also one that he did not have to make for, as he stood there undecided, the wardrobe door was pushed open, slowly, from inside.

"I hope you realize you are trespassing on private property?"

The man who spoke, and who had just stepped out of the wardrobe, was tall, thin, and had a long pale face with a sad expression. His black hair was swept back smoothly from his high forehead and his eyes were red-rimmed. He wore a black suit and a starched white shirt with a black bow-tie. There was

a gold medallion on a chain around his neck and, over his shoulders, a scarlet-lined black cloak.

There could be no mistaking his identity.

"I know who you are," said Henry, in as firm a voice as he could muster. He took a tight hold of the garlic bulb in his pocket.

"Don't change the subject," said the sad-faced man and, as he spoke, his long, thin fingers fluttered delicately in the air.

"You're Count Dracula," said Henry.

"No, I'm not," said the man.

"Yes, you are! There's no need to lie about it."

"I'm *not* lying," said the man. "I am a count, yes. But I'm not Count Dracula. I'm Count Alucard."

"'Alucard'," said Henry, "is 'Dracula' backwards."

"Is it really?" said the man. "Goodness me, I'd never noticed!"

Henry knew there was one sure way of proving whether or not the man was a vampire. He pulled the garlic bulb from out of his pocket and brandished it under the man's nose.

"Don't do that," said the count, taking a step backwards in alarm.

"There you are!" said Henry. "That settles it!"

"Settles what?"

"It proves you're Count Dracula," said Henry. "It proves you're a vampire."

"It doesn't prove anything of the kind," replied the count, tartly. "It proves I don't like garlic, that's all. Lots of people don't like garlic, but it doesn't mean that they're all vampires. Do *you* like garlic?"

Henry shook his head. "Not very much," he admitted.

"And are *you* a vampire?"

"Of course not!" said Henry, grinning at the idea.

"Well then! You haven't proved anything at all. Are there other things you like less than garlic?"

Henry thought for a moment and then nodded. "I'm not very fond of cabbage," he said. "Especially school-dinner cabbage."

"And how would you like it, young man, if I waved a handful of school-dinner cabbage under *your* nose—like you did to me with the garlic?"

"Not very much," admitted Henry, and added: "I'm very sorry."

"So you should be," said the count and then, relenting slightly, he added: "I forgive you—this time."

"But if you *aren't* Count Dracula, why are you hiding in this castle on your own?" asked Henry. "And why do you keep all the doors and windows locked and barred?"

The count paused, then changed the subject. "Do you like violin music?" he said.

Henry who, to tell the truth, could take it or leave it alone, shrugged. "Sometimes," he said.

"Good!" said the count. He turned the record over on the turntable, wound the handle, and replaced the needle in the groove. The soft strains of the violin settled on the air once more. The count listened, his head on one side, a wistful look on his face, for several seconds, and then he looked hard at Henry, as though wondering whether or not to tell him something. At last, he did. "We changed our name, you know," he said.

"From Dracula to Alucard?" asked Henry.

The count nodded. "My grandfather was the last of the Draculas. *All* of my ancestors were Draculas. They're lying in a tomb somewhere in the castle grounds. Or at least their skeletons are. In their coffins. They've all got wooden stakes thrust through their hearts—did you know that was the only way to kill a vampire?"

Henry nodded. He had seen it happen once on the telly in a late-night horror film. "And if anyone ever takes the stake away," he said, "the vampire comes back to life again."

Count Alucard nodded. "My ancestors won't ever come back to life again," he said. "Nobody knows where they're buried. Not even me. It's a secret. They've lain dead and forgotten all these years. . ." He paused, sighed, and then added: "Dead and forgotten, all of the Draculas!"

"Do you mean," asked Henry, "that you don't change into a vampire and go round biting people's necks and sucking their blood?"

The count pulled a face. "Certainly not!" he said. "What a dreadful thought! I do change into a bat occasionally—but I wouldn't *dream* of sucking anyone's blood. As a matter of fact, I'm a vegetarian."

Henry laughed. "Whoever heard of a vegetarian vampire?" he said.

"Did you ever hear of a fruit-eating bat?" said the count.

"Well—yes," admitted Henry.

"I change into one of those," said the count, and then his face lit up. "I *love* oranges," he said. "I don't turn my nose up at a plum or the odd banana, but I'm simply *mad* about oranges. I don't suppose you've got one in your pocket, by any chance?"

Henry shook his head. "Only the garlic bulb," he said.

"Forget it," said the count, pulling another face.

"But I still don't understand," said Henry. "If you *don't* go around terrorizing the countryside and causing mayhem, why do you have to hide yourself away in here?"

"Where else could I go? It's the only place I know," said the count. He jerked his head to where the mountain lay beyond the castle wall, and continued: "And I've got to keep my living here a secret because of them."

"Who's them?" asked Henry.

"There's a whole village full of people just round the mountain. Superstitious lot! If they got so much as a whisper that I was in the district, they'd come charging up with hayforks and scythes and that sort of thing—anything sharp or pointed they could lay their hands on."

"But *why*?" asked Henry, puzzled. "What *for*?"

"Because it's their nature," said Count Alucard, gloomily.

"But surely if you explained to them?" said Henry. "About your being a vegetarian?"

"Explained to *them*!" Count Alucard let out a hollow laugh. "They wouldn't give me a chance to explain anything. They'd have a wooden stake through my heart before you could say 'Frankenstein's monster'." Count Alucard sighed again and his long pale fingers fluttered sadly. "It gets very lonely sometimes—being a vampire," he said.

"I bet it does," said Henry. "I do wish I could help."

Count Alucard and Henry sat lost in their own thoughts. The gramophone had finished playing some time before, but neither of them seemed to notice that the music had come to an end. The record was still revolving, slowly now, on the turntable. The only sound was that of the needle scratching, noisily, in the groove.

5

It was well past mid-day. The sun was high in the sky. It was very hot inside the village hall which was packed to the doors. Every single villager was present and those who could not find a chair to sit on were standing round the walls of the room while others even clung to the rafters.

The heat was making them bad-tempered and it seemed as if they were all shouting at once.

"What we need are hayforks!" called one villager.

"And scythes!" called another.

"Anything we can lay our hands on that is sharp or pointed!" cried a third.

While up on the platform, a short, round man banged his fist on the green-baize-covered table, demanding silence. "Quiet! *Quiet!* All of you!" shouted Henri Rumboll who, as well as being the mayor, was also the village postmaster. "We are here to decide what we're going to do! There's no sense in panicking!"

"It's all very well you telling us not to panic," cried a bearded villager from the rear of the hall, "but some of us are old enough to remember the last time there was trouble at the castle!"

His words were greeted with a roar of approval from most of his fellow villagers.

"We don't know that there *will* be trouble at the castle!" replied the mayor.

"*We* don't know anything at all!" snapped a tight-lipped red-headed woman who was sitting in the front row holding a bundle of washing. "That's what most of us are complaining about," she continued. "We were told there was a meeting in the village hall, nothing else. We know nothing apart from ugly rumours about a stranger and the Castle Alucard."

Angry murmurs rose from around the hall, agreeing with the woman.

"That's exactly why you were summoned here," put in the mayor, quickly, attempting to calm the meeting. "To keep you informed!" He turned and looked down at Alphonse Kropotel who was sitting next to him on the platform. "Our sergeant of police told me what had happened and I immediately called this meeting."

"But what *has* happened, Henri Rumboll?" demanded the red-haired woman, rising to her feet still clutching her washing. "That's what we want to know!"

"Yes!" called another villager. "Is it true that it's a job for hayforks?"

"Should I run back to my farm and fetch my scythe?" shouted another.

"Should we start to collect together all the sharp and pointed things we can lay our hands on?" cried a third.

"Tell us! Tell us!" called the mass of villagers in the hall.

The mayor, unable to make himself heard above the din, shrugged hopelessly and sat down.

Sergeant Kropotel rose to his feet and hammered on the table with his swagger-stick. "If order is not restored to this room at once," he shouted, "I shall fine each and every one of you ten gumbeks for causing a disturbance!"

The villagers fell silent.

"Good!" said the sergeant of police. "Now then, the situation is as follows: a stranger arrived this morning in the village and let it be known that he was staying in the vicinity of the Castle Alucard."

A gasp of horror went up from the villagers at this confirmation, at last, of a rumour that they had hoped against hope had been unfounded.

"Not only that," continued Kropotel, "but it would seem that he has also been using several identities!"

The shopkeeper who, in his haste to get to the meeting, had not had time to take off his apron, rose to his feet. "He came into my shop, spoke in English, and ordered half a kilo of cheese—it's still sitting on my counter if any of you want to have a look at it!"

The old man who had been sitting on the bench in the cobbled square clambered to his feet and waved his empty pipe in the air to attract attention. "The stranger came across to me and spoke in French!" he said.

The old woman who had been plucking the goose and the duck and who was now sitting on the end of a row of seats with a half-plucked chicken between her knees, spoke up through a cloud of feathers. "The stranger came across and talked to me in German!" she said.

The villagers muttered to each other, anxiously. It was quite obvious to them all that, whoever the stranger was, he was certainly not up to any good.

"It is my opinion," said Sergeant Kropotel, "that the whole business of the stranger demands a full investigation. Any man who adopts three different identities in one morning needs his credentials looking into—" He broke off and looked across at a plump woman with apple-cheeks who had been trying to attract his attention. "Yes, Greta? What is it?" he said.

"The stranger came across to me, while I was feeding my hens, and spoke to me in Italian," said the apple-cheeked woman.

There were more gasps of dismay from the villagers.

Sergeant Kropotel's mouth dropped open. The fact that the stranger had also pretended to be an Italian came as a complete shock to him. He hammered again with his swagger-stick on the table. "You see, friends?" he said. "The situation gets more serious every moment!"

"While we sit here and do nothing but talk about it!" snapped the red-headed woman with the bundle of washing.

"The washerwoman's right!" It was a large black-haired unshaven man with bulging muscles who had got to his feet. "You're quick enough to act, Sergeant, when one of us leaves his horse and cart for a minute too long on the village square! What are you going to do about this business—now?"

"*I'll* tell you what the sergeant of police is going to do!" It was the mayor, Henri Rumboll, who had got to his feet again,

feeling it was high time he had another word or two. "He's going to the Castle Alucard to seek out this stranger for himself and then interrogate him thoroughly. Aren't you, Sergeant?"

Kropotel swallowed, hastily. He hadn't intended *quite* such drastic action. "Am I?" he murmured.

"Of course! We must settle the question, once and for all, as to whether the stranger is flesh or fiend and, if our suspicions prove correct, our brave sergeant of police will do his duty!" In order to illustrate his point, the mayor hammered at an imaginary wooden stake with an imaginary mallet.

This was the sort of stuff the villagers wanted to hear! They rose to their feet as one man, and cheered and cheered.

Sergeant Kropotel licked at his dry lips as he listened to the applause. It was all right for *them*, he thought. It was all right for the mayor, too, telling him what to do. But in order to get to the Castle Alucard it would be necessary to travel through the dark pine-forest. There was then the question of the wolf-pack. The terrible beasts of the forest! And, supposing he managed to dodge the wolves and found the stranger and confronted him, what would he say? "Excuse me, sir, but I have reason to believe that you may be a vampire. Would you mind lying down while I hammer this wooden stake through your heart?" Ah, if only it were that easy!

With the cheers of the villagers still ringing in the rafters, Kropotel turned to the mayor. "Surely you don't expect me to go alone?" he whispered.

The mayor considered the question and then held up his hands for silence. "Sergeant Kropotel will require a volunteer to go with him," he said. "I know that each and every man amongst you will be eager to take on the task—and so, in order that there be no arguments, how would it be if you draw lots for it?"

The villagers mulled over the suggestion and didn't appear to be too keen on the idea. While they were still ruminating, Eric Horowitz, the shopkeeper, got to his feet. "I propose," he said, "that we allow our gallant mayor himself, Henri Rumboll, the honour of accompanying the police-sergeant!"

"I second that!" It was the black-haired unshaven man who had jumped quickly to his feet.

"No, no," began the mayor, "I couldn't let you—" but his words were drowned by another burst of cheering from the villagers.

Kropotel smiled to himself. It served the old fool right, he thought. After all, it was his own fault.

"That's settled then," announced the police-sergeant. "The mayor and myself will set off for the Castle Alucard immediately after lunch!"

"God bless and protect you both!" cried the red-headed washerwoman.

The meeting broke up to still more tumultuous applause.

"Does anybody want to buy a fine, plump, oven-ready chicken?" called the old woman, holding up a pink plucked carcase as the villagers streamed towards the doors.

"A *count*? A *real* count?" asked Emily Hollins. "Coming here for his tea?"

Henry nodded. "His name's Count Alucard," he said. "And he said he'd very much like to meet you."

Emily, flustered, fiddled with her back hair and glanced across at Albert who was tightening guy-ropes round the tent.

"Well," she simpered, coyly, "I've no objection to him having tea with us in the tent, if it's all right with your father?"

Albert Hollins, on his knees, glanced up. "I don't know about him having tea in the tent," he grumbled. "He'll be lucky if the blooming thing doesn't fall down on him! I don't know who keeps losing all our tent-pegs. If you ask me, we must have left a trail of them right across Europe! Either that, or somebody's been eating them!"

Emily sniffed, huffily. "If it was left to somebody whose name I *could* mention, but won't, we might have nothing at all to eat *but* tent-pegs."

Albert glanced up, sharply. "It wasn't my fault, you know, that I couldn't get any food in the village," he said. "You try going up and see if you can do any better. They're all crackers up there! I wasn't going to stand around in that village shop and be made a fool of."

"You must have done something to deserve it," said Emily.

"All I did was ask for half a kilo of cheese. The next thing I know, the shopkeeper's done a bunk and he's spying on me through a keyhole!"

Emily shook her head, disbelievingly. "That's your story, Albert," she said. "But it's left me in a bit of a pickle! Here I am, with a real live foreign count coming for his tea—and I've nothing in the tent to offer him but tinned stuff."

Albert, having completed his inspection of the tent, rose and dusted his hands together. "I suppose he'll take us as he finds us," he said.

"It's not a question of taking us as he finds us," retorted Emily. "It's a question of good manners." She turned to Henry. "Have you any ideas about what I ought to offer him?"

"Not really," replied Henry. "Although he did mention that he's a vegetarian." It crossed Henry's mind that he ought to tell his parents that, as well as being a vegetarian, Count Alucard was also a vampire, but he decided some things were better left unsaid.

"Oh dear!" sighed Emily. "If he's a vegetarian that means I'd better cross the corned beef sandwiches off my menu!"

"But I do know that he's very fond of fruit," said Henry.

"Good! I'll open another tin of peaches then," said Emily and, turning to Albert, she added: "You won't say 'no' to them twice in one day, I don't suppose?"

Albert smiled, smugly, and shook his head. Tinned peaches were his favourite food and he would have tucked into them, quite happily, had Emily served them up for every meal.

Emily Hollins ticked off items on her fingers as she spoke. "That's tinned peaches; tinned cream; tinned chocolate finger biscuits and tinned strawberry and apple jam," she said, and then frowned. "Does that sound like a suitable spread for a representative of the European aristocracy?" she asked.

"Sounds fine to me," said Henry, who was quite sure Count Alucard would not mind what was offered to him. The vegetarian vampire had leapt at the invitation out to tea with the Hollins family but, Henry felt sure, the lonely count was coming more for the company than the food.

"What time did he say he'd be presenting his compliments?" asked Albert, proud at having the right word for the occasion —ordinary folk roll up for tea, but lords and ladies, as Albert knew, present their compliments.

"Tea-time," answered Henry, "about half past four, he said."

"It's high time he was putting in an appearance then," said Albert, hungrily eyeing the tinned peaches. He dragged his gaze away from the food and looked across towards the castle. He blinked, twice. "Well, I'll be blowed!" he said.

"What is it, Albert?" asked Emily, busily arranging chocolate finger biscuits in a dainty pattern on a plastic plate.

"I think you'd better set a couple more places at the table," said Albert. "It looks as if we've got *more* visitors!"

"Where?" said Emily.

"I can't see anybody," said Henry.

"There!" said Albert. "Coming down the mountain—a couple of blinking mountaineers!"

From where the Hollins family were standing, the two figures, roped together, and making an unsteady progress around and down the side of the mountain, might have looked like a couple of *bona fide* mountaineers. But a closer inspection would have revealed their true identities—they were Police-Sergeant Kropotel and Mayor Rumboll from the mountain village.

Henri Rumboll caught at his breath and then gasped as he almost lost his footing and sent a shower of loose stones cascading down the mountainside.

"This idea of yours, to come down the mountain instead of through the forest, is one of the most hare-brained, crack-pot schemes I've ever come across!" panted the mayor, glancing down at Kropotel who was just below him, leading the way.

Kropotel looked up but all he could see were the soles of Rumboll's mayoral boots. "It's a matter of opinion, Henri," he grunted. "But, speaking personally, I'd rather take my chances on this mountainside than tangle in the forest with those wolves!"

Sergeant Kropotel shifted his swagger-stick from underneath one arm to underneath the other, and wished that he'd had the good sense to leave it in the station. As well as his stick, the police-sergeant was also responsible for carrying the half kilo of cheese that Albert Hollins had purchased in the village shop and which was, at that moment, dangling from his shoulder in a package. Delivering the cheese to Albert was to be Kropotel's excuse for paying the stranger and his family a visit. The police-sergeant swore to himself under his breath, as the string that held the package of cheese got twisted round his swagger-stick.

"How much further have we got to go?" asked Rumboll, afraid to look down.

"Not far now!" called Kropotel, then: *"Ouch!"* he added, as the toe of Rumboll's right boot landed fair and square on the fingertips of his outstretched left hand. "Look where you're putting your big feet!"

From which point on, both Sergeant Kropotel and Mayor Rumboll lapsed into silence as they concentrated all their attentions on the difficult task of getting themselves to ground level with their bones intact.

Albert Hollins was not the only person to have spotted the two men clinging to the mountainside.

Count Alucard was just about to buckle his red-lined cloak over his shoulders when he also caught sight of Kropotel and Rumboll from one of the castle's windows. And not only did he see them, he recognized them immediately for what they were.

"Villagers!" muttered the count to himself. Just when he was about to go out for tea, too! Well, so much for his little outing. There was no way that he could pay his visit to the Hollins while there were villagers in the area. Whenever there was so much as a sniff of villagers anywhere near the castle, Count Alucard kept a very low profile indeed. He usually hid in the wardrobe. He wondered what these two wanted. He hadn't seen any villagers around for years.

"They're sure to have come here vampire-hunting," he said to himself. Count Alucard let out a longsuffering sigh. There was nothing in all the world that he disliked so much as vampire-hunters. Prowling round the district with crosses hanging from their necks and their pockets stuffed with garlic bulbs!

"If I had a gumbek for every garlic bulb that's been carried round this castle," said Count Alucard to himself, "I'd be a very rich vampire indeed!"

It had to be admitted, of course, that Henry Hollins, his new-found friend, had first arrived with a garlic bulb in his pocket—but he, at least, had had the good manners to get rid

74

of it when asked. *And* he'd apologized. You wouldn't catch a villager apologizing to a vampire! Not even to a vegetarian vampire! Not in a month of full moons.

"More likely to drive a wooden stake through your heart first, and ask questions afterwards!" the count muttered to himself, as he crept inside the wardrobe and quietly closed the door.

6

Having successfully completed their descent of the mountain, and after pausing only momentarily to examine their elbows and knees for minor cuts and bruises, Alphonse Kropotel and Henri Rumboll struck out, giving the dark and silent castle a wide berth, down the grassy slope towards where the Hollins' tent was pitched.

"Better leave all the talking to me, Henri," said Kropotel, one hand holding the end of the swagger-stick which was tucked, firmly, under his armpit while his other hand clutched, for security, at a couple of garlic bulbs in his pocket.

Henri Rumboll nervously fingered the heavy silver cross he was wearing, for protection, on a cord around his neck. "Whatever you say, Sergeant," said the mayor, only too happy to be as little involved as possible.

Inside the tent, Albert Hollins peered at the two tiny figures in the distance. "Well, I'll be jiggered!" he said. "They are coming here. Straight towards us."

"Who are they, Albert?" said Emily.

"Search me," said Albert. "Looks like an official visit though—one of 'em's wearing a uniform."

"What kind of uniform?" asked Emily.

76

Albert shrugged. "Dunno," he said. "But there's enough gold braid on it for a major-general!" He paused, and added: "Funny sort of get-up to go mountaineering in!"

"Counts! Major-generals! My goodness me, we do see life!" said Emily, blissfully. But the smile soon faded from her face as she caught sight of a pan in a corner of the tent which held the remains of their last meal. "Albert Hollins!" she said. "I distinctly remember asking you to get rid of that!"

"Sorry, Emily," said Albert, half on his feet.

"Don't bother!" she snapped. "I'll see to it. If you want anything doing in this tent, you're better off doing it yourself!" With which she picked up the offending pan containing the remnants of the stew and slipped out through the tent-doors.

Kropotel and Rumboll spotted the figure leaving the tent, carrying the pan and heading for the perimeter of the pine-forest.

"Who's that?" asked Rumboll.

"That'll be the stranger's wife," replied the police-sergeant, tapping the side of his polished boot with his swagger-stick as he strode along.

"Do you mean that he's not *alone*?" The news came as something of a shock to the mayor.

Kropotel shook his head. "No. According to the story he told the shopkeeper, he's here with his wife and son."

Mayor Rumboll was horrified. "Nobody told *me* that," he said. "Why, it means that we could be dealing with not one but three vam—" He broke off and his eyes widened with terror. "Merciful heaven!" he murmured.

A huge grey-brown shape had come hurtling out of the pine-trees. It was followed, closely, by a similar but even larger grey-brown shape.

The police-sergeant and the mayor watched, open-mouthed, as the pair of lean and hungry wolves sped across the grassy slopes.

"Don't move!" hissed Kropotel through clenched teeth. "Stand perfectly still!"

The instructions were totally unnecessary. Henri Rumboll could not have moved an inch had he so desired. He was rooted to the spot with fear.

Across the grassy slope, standing closer to the edge of the forest, Emily Hollins was quite delighted to renew her acquaintance with the big Alsatian. "Good doggie!" she burbled. "Who's a clever-*clever* doggie then? And have you brought a little doggie friend with you? *Yes*, you have! You have!"

The first wolf bared its ugly fangs, raised its head, snarled, and then let out a long, low, menacing growl.

The second wolf watched its fellow's behaviour, curiously. Not without reason was the second wolf the leader of the entire pack. It was the craftiest wolf in the forest. On the previous day, it had noticed the first wolf come slinking back from an expedition looking furtive, well fed, and obviously hugging some secret to itself. The wolf-pack leader had resolved, there and then, to keep a watchful eye on the wandering pack-member. If there was some sort of hidden supply of food to be found, the wolf-pack leader considered it had a natural right to be in on things. The plan was now about to pay dividends. The first wolf had led it to a succulent, juicy human! But why, wondered the pack-leader, wasn't the first wolf helping itself to a tender arm or a tasty leg? The wolf-pack leader, puzzled, cocked its head on one side and waited for developments. It was not kept waiting long.

"Here, doggies! Good doggies!" said Emily, dipping a wooden spoon into the remains of the corned beef stew and tossing morsels in the direction of both animals.

The wolves gobbled them down, instantly.

Ambrosia!

Incredibly delicious!

Even the first wolf was forced to admit to itself that what it had just tasted was far superior to the cubes of meat served the day before. Cold corned beef had been delight enough, but swallowed down now, with benefit of thick gravy and peas and beans and potatoes and carrots. . . How had it managed to exist so long, the wolf wondered, without ever sampling such delicacies?

The second wolf was experiencing a similar sensation. It would never so much as look at a stringy rabbit-leg again! The wolf-pack leader understood now why the first wolf hadn't bitten lumps out of the human person. If the human person were to ask the pack-leader to jump through a blazing hoop for a second mouthful of that delicious concoction, it would not hesitate for an instant.

But Emily Hollins made no such demands upon the creatures. "Here, doggies! Nice doggies! Have some stewsy-wewsy!" she trilled, tossing them a second helping of mouth-watering tit-bits.

And, from that moment on, the wolves were Emily's dedicated slaves for life.

Across the slope and towards the castle, Alphonse Kropotel and Henri Rumboll allowed themselves to breathe again as it slowly dawned on them that they were not about to be eaten by wolves. There was hope yet! They could not, at that distance,

hear what the stranger's wife was saying to the two huge beasts and, truth to tell, they were not particularly interested. The only thing that concerned them was that the wolves' attention was not on them.

"I think perhaps it's high time we were making a move, Henri," whispered the police-sergeant.

"A good idea," muttered the mayor. "I certainly think we've seen all we need to see here!"

They set off, slowly at first and walking backwards, keeping their eyes fixed on the fierce creatures that were still snuffling and scuffling at Emily's feet. Then, when they felt themselves to be far enough away for safety, they turned and took to their heels, back in the direction from which they had first come.

Inside the tent, Albert and Henry, both unaware of Emily's contact with the wolves, watched the two villagers running hell-for-leather towards the mountain.

"That's funny!" said Albert. "It doesn't look as if those two coves are going to pay us a visit after all. I wonder where they're off to in such a hurry?"

"Dunno, Dad," said Henry. "What time is it?"

Albert glanced at his watch. "Nearly five o'clock, lad. It doesn't look as though that count of yours is going to put in an appearance either."

"No," said Henry, sadly. "It doesn't, does it?"

Albert Hollins rubbed his hands together, briskly. "Not to worry," he said. "I should think you and me between us can manage these tinned peaches!"

The next sound to be heard in the tent was that of Albert Hollins, chomping steadily.

Police-Sergeant Kropotel and Mayor Rumboll did not have much to say to each other either. They were far too busy scrambling back up and round the mountain to pause for conversation. Oddly enough, they managed somehow to get up the mountain far quicker than they had come down. And not until they were standing safely on the other side and gazing down on the peace and quiet of their village did they stop, first to regain their breath, and then to speak.

"My God!" murmured the mayor. "Did you see the sheer *size* of those vicious brutes!"

"And their fangs!"

"And their claws!"

"*And* that woman standing there as happy as you please and chatting to them as if. . ." the police-sergeant paused and groped for words, " . . . as if they were mere puppy-dogs!"

The mayor nodded. "At least it's served to confirm our suspicions," he said.

"Oh, they're a family of vampires all right—without a shadow of doubt. No human person would ever consort with wolves."

The mayor nodded, gravely. "The next thing to be decided, Sergeant," he said, "is what are you going to do about it?"

Kropotel shuffled, uneasily. He did not like the way in which the entire problem had suddenly been shifted on to his shoulders. "I think," he said, "that this calls for another meeting of the villagers."

"Oh?"

"Yes. It's my opinion that what's needed now is sheer weight of numbers. It's not a job for one man. I think we should all go back there—every single villager. In force. It's the only way to tackle vampires."

"You really think so?"

"I'm sure of it."

"Oh." It was not a suggestion that appealed overmuch to the mayor, who had been secretly hoping that the sergeant of police would have been able to cope with the problem alone. "Were you thinking of going back there today?" he asked.

Kropotel scratched his beard. He was hot. He was dusty. His uniform needed brushing down. His boots could do with a good polish. It had been a long, hard day. What he needed most of all was a good night's rest. He tapped his swagger-stick on the side of his boot and gave the matter due consideration. There was no sense, it seemed, in rushing into things. All actions appertaining to vampires and wolves were worthy of a lot of thought. "No, not today," he said at last. "We'll summon a meeting in the village hall tomorrow morning."

The mayor nodded. Tomorrow sounded like a good idea to him too. "You're right, Sergeant," he said. "We mustn't be too hasty in this matter. And the villagers will need to arm themselves, of course."

"Of course."

"Hayforks and scythes, that sort of thing. Anything else they can lay their hands on that is sharp or pointed."

"Of course," repeated Kropotel.

"And we will need to take some wooden stakes and a mallet along as well," said the mayor, and added: "For you know what. . ." And he mimed the action of driving a wooden stake through a vampire's heart.

"A mallet and a wooden stake will certainly come in very useful," said Kropotel.

Later that night, long after both Albert and Henry were fast asleep, Emily Hollins lay awake in her sleeping-bag staring through a gap in the tent-doors at the bright stars in the clear night sky. She had tossed this way and that and even tried to take her mind off things by browsing through a couple of travel brochures by the light of the moon. But it was no use. Emily was very worried.

Her concern was for the well-being of the two big guard dogs which, she was sure, were not being given the care and attention that they needed and deserved. Poor things! They were so lean and hungry. And as for grooming—why, their coats didn't look as if they'd even *seen* a brush in years! She had not mentioned her meeting with the animals to either her husband or her son because, she knew, they would only have laughed at her as they always did when they felt she was fussing over things that didn't concern her. But, whether they liked it or not, it was Emily's nature to fuss—and particularly where animals were concerned.

It was a pity, thought Emily, that Henry's friend, Count What's-his-name, hadn't turned up for tea as he had said he would. She would certainly have taken up the subject of the dogs with him, count or no count! All right, perhaps the upkeep of the castle's guard dogs was the concern of the count's servants and not himself—but surely it was up to the count to see that his staff did their jobs properly? Yes, if only the count had arrived for tea as promised, Emily would certainly have given him a piece of her mind. . .

Suddenly, she had a brilliant idea. There was nothing to stop her, was there, from going up to the castle the next morning, confronting the count, and telling him just what she thought? Nothing at all. Albert and Henry would try to talk her out of going, but supposing she set off very early, before either of them had woken up? Yes, resolved Emily, that was exactly what she would do. Then, having satisfactorily solved the matter in her mind, she snuggled down in her sleeping-bag and promptly fell fast asleep.

Had she lain awake a few moments longer she would have heard again the sad song of a violin carried across from the castle on the sighing wind.

Count Alucard was also finding it difficult to get to sleep. He too had problems on his mind and he was playing his gramophone records in an attempt to ease his worries. But, try as he would, the count could not forget the two villagers he had spotted climbing down the mountainside that afternoon. He had spent most of the evening and much of the night hidden in the wardrobe for fear that the villagers might enter the castle and discover him. It had not been comfortable inside the wardrobe. He had had pins and needles in his right shoulder and cramp in his left foot. The villagers had not come inside the castle, it was true, but Count Alucard had an uneasy feeling that he had not seen the last of them. What was worse, he had the unhappy feeling that if the villagers *did* return, they would come back in force.

Count Alucard shook his head, sorrowfully, and examined the nails on the end of his pale, slim fingers.

When the count had been a small boy, his father had often perched him on his knee and recounted stories about the bad old days when the castle was constantly being besieged by villagers who came carrying blazing torches and brandishing hayforks, scythes and suchlike dangerous weapons. Count Alucard had no desire to excuse the exploits of his blood-drinking ancestors—all the same, he did feel that peasants who

85

went around the countryside with the sole intention of bashing wooden stakes through people's hearts deserved everything they got in return. Although he was not himself a bloodsucking vampire, if anyone ever came after him with a sharp stake and a large mallet, he decided, he would not be averse, as a last resort, to giving them a quick nip with his sharp teeth. . .

The count sighed. He was not by nature a violent man—in fact, if anything, he was quite the reverse. If only he had been born elsewhere. . . If only he had not been put upon the earth as a vampire. . . If only he didn't have to carry the sins of his forebears upon his cloaked shoulders. . . If only. . .

The violin music came to an end. Count Alucard pulled himself out of his reverie, replaced the record on the gramophone turntable with another, then leaned back in the solitary comfort of his room and attempted, yet again, to lose himself in the pleasure of the music.

7

Emily Hollins drew back her arm and then threw the stick as far as she could. "Fetch it! Fetch, fetch!" she cried.

The wolves sat down, puzzled, and gazed at her, unblinking. There were now three of them. The two that had previously presented themselves had been joined by a savage, rangy she-wolf—the pack-leader's mate.

Emily, true to her own resolve of the night before, had crawled, yawning, out of her sleeping-bag while Albert and Henry slumbered on. When Emily arose it was so early, in fact, that even the wolf-pack was still fast asleep in the dark of the forest—asleep, that is, with the exception of the pack-leader and the first wolf who had both spent the night with one eye each half cocked on the tent that lay beyond the pine-forest. The she-wolf too, her suspicions aroused by her mate's absence on the previous afternoon, had slept with one eye half open. The vigilance of all three of them had been rewarded when, with the sun barely over the mountain peak, they had spotted Emily emerging from the tent.

Emily Hollins had not been at all surprised to see three guard dogs instead of two come padding towards her. "What's your name, then? Eh? Eh?" she had enquired of the latest arrival.

The she-wolf, like her companions before her, had been somewhat taken aback at the strange behaviour of the human. And, again as her companions had done, she had sniffed hungrily and licked her chops at the appetizing hand that was held out towards her. But before the she-wolf could snatch at golden opportunity and chew off a couple of meaty fingers, Emily's hand had moved on past the beast's slavering jaws and taken a firm grip on one of its ears.

"Who's a good girl then?" said Emily, cheerfully. "Who's a good doggie? Who's Auntie Emily's good old pal?"

The she-wolf had growled, menacingly, at this treatment and looked towards both of its companions for a sign that they were about to pounce on the wretched human and tear it limb from limb. But, oddly, both the first wolf and the pack-leader had stood quietly on either side, heads cocked and tails wagging, as Emily tugged and pulled at the she-wolf's ears. Realizing that there must be more to the situation than immediately met the eye, the she-wolf decided to follow her companions' behaviour, for the time being at least, and allow events to take their course.

"Come on then, doggies!" Emily had said, turning and striding off across the grassy slope. "*Walkies!*"

Upon which command, both the first wolf and the wolf-pack leader had padded off, obediently, at the heels of the human.

Of course! The she-wolf had realized at last the game that the other two were playing. Why hadn't she seen through it before? It was their intention, obviously, to wait until they were well out of earshot of the pine-forest before leaping on the human and ripping it to shreds. That way they would not have to share the feast with the rest of the ravenous wolf-pack. They would have it all to themselves. Very well. All right. If that was the plan the she-wolf was only too happy to go along with it. There was more than enough flesh on the human for all three of them. There would be no need to snarl and snap and squabble, as was usual at every meal, over which of them got what. The she-wolf licked her lips again in happy anticipation of what would certainly turn out to be the finest meal she had had in years and set off in the wake of her companions.

Emily was in no hurry. She did not profess to know a great deal about the lifestyles of those fortunate folk that dwelt in castles, but she was quite sure that it was not their normal practice to get up at the crack of dawn. She had decided, therefore, that she would take the dogs on a ramble around the countryside before presenting herself at the castle gates and demanding to see the count.

In her mind, she rehearsed, over and over again, the speech that she would deliver to him about the proper care, food, and attention that should be given to our four-footed friends. In her handbag were two tins of corned beef which she was taking along to show him as an example of the kind of meat to which his dogs were partial. Emily also intended to point out to the count that he really ought to keep his pets under some sort of control. It wasn't fair on either the dogs themselves *or* the general public to allow them to wander about, at all hours, all over the countryside. Emily, as a dog-lover, could see that they were harmless, lovable household animals—but supposing someone not quite as knowledgeable were to suddenly chance on a couple of them scampering in the forest? Why—an old-age pensioner, for instance, might quite easily be frightened out of his wits! And why weren't the dogs wearing regulation collars and name-tags? Oh yes, there was a great deal that Emily intended to take the count to task about.

She walked across and picked up the stick which she had thrown and which the dogs were showing little enthusiasm for. She waved the stick under the pack-leader's nose. "Here, boy! Smell! Smell, boy!" she said.

The wolf-pack leader sniffed at the stick disdainfully, unable to understand why the human kept thrusting the piece of wood in its face. And why, also, it wondered, did the human keep throwing the piece of wood away and then go chasing after it? But then, nothing the human did made sense. The pack-leader turned its head away from the stick, thoroughly bored with the whole procedure.

Emily too was tiring of the sport—if sport it was. There was little fun, she was finding, in throwing a stick and then having

to do the retrieving oneself. It was becoming increasingly obvious to Emily that no one had taken the trouble to teach any of the dogs anything at all! Not one of them, she had discovered, showed any aptitude for any of the usual doggy tricks: *Sitting*, for example, or *Begging*, or *Rolling Over*, or even *Lying Down for the Queen*. And now the entire trio refused point-blank to perform that simplest of canine tasks and bring back a stick that had been thrown for them. Well, she would give them one more chance.

Drawing back her arm once again, she launched the stick into the air. The three wolves hardly raised an eyebrow as the stick rose, then dipped, and finally dropped into a patch of undergrowth.

"Fetch it! Fetch, fetch!" bellowed Emily for the umpteenth time. Then, in order to give the animals an idea of what was

expected of them, she sprinted after the stick, head down, into the very heart of the undergrowth.

The three wolves followed Emily's progress with complete disinterest. One of them yawned, another stretched itself, while the third lifted a mangy paw and scratched, lazily, at a persistent flea behind its right ear. All three, however, sat bolt upright and took notice as, suddenly, the earth appeared to open and Emily, with no more than a sharp gasp of surprise, disappeared from sight. The wolves blinked, exchanged puzzled glances, and then padded over towards the spot where Emily had performed her mysterious vanishing trick.

A large hole, previously hidden in the thick tangle of undergrowth, marked the point at which Emily had entered the bowels of the earth. The wolves craned their necks and peered down into the blackness of the hole. Emily, some twelve feet below, peered back at them.

As she had felt the ground give way beneath her, Emily had grasped out, wildly, with both her hands, but there was nothing to hold on to and she felt herself scrabbling at air. She had landed with a painful bump which took her breath away. But on scrambling to her feet and gingerly feeling herself all over, she was relieved to discover that she did not appear to have suffered any serious injury. Glancing around into the darkness that loomed in on all sides, she realized that she was in some sort of underground chamber. Then, looking up instinctively towards the only source of light that filtered through the hole by which she had entered, Emily was further reassured to see her three companions, the guard dogs, peering down at her.

"Good dogs! Good boys!" said Emily, encouragingly.

The wolves gazed back at her, uncomprehending.

Emily's thoughts raced. She was in urgent need of help. It was quite impossible for her to climb out of the underground chamber without some human assistance. She had wandered far too far from the camp-site for any shouts to be heard by her immediate family. No, if aid were to be summoned quickly then she must look to her faithful four-footed friends.

"Fetch help!" she called up at the wolves. "Go to the castle! Bring your master!"

The wolves stared down, unblinking.

"Quickly! *Please!*" urged Emily, beseechingly.

The wolf-pack leader was the first to turn and lope off across the countryside. There was little point in hanging about at the top of the hole, he had decided. The human was hardly likely to throw food up at him. No, if the aching pangs of hunger that were gnawing at his stomach were ever to be satisfied, then he must needs look elsewhere for sustenance. A possibility had occurred to him. With luck, he might just pounce upon an early venturing rabbit—always provided that he was first wolf at the rabbit-holes that morning. The pack-leader increased his pace as he heard the panting of his two companions who were fast arriving at his heels. The first wolf and the she-wolf had come to the same tempting decision as the wolf-pack leader.

Back in the underground chamber, Emily Hollins let out a small sigh of relief. It was good to know that help would soon be on its way. Until it came, and now that her eyes were becoming accustomed to the gloom, she decided to spend the time in examining her surroundings. Emily smiled to herself. She had just thought of something else that she would point out to the count when she came face to face with him: be good and loving to your pets and, certainly, they will repay kindness with kindness.

Out in the open countryside, the three lean wolves raced each other, neck and neck, with all thoughts of Emily totally dismissed from their minds, towards the rabbit-warrens that lay beyond the farthest fringe of the pine-forest.

Mayor Henri Rumboll balanced himself, unsteadily, on the narrow stone surround which supported the ancient cross in the cobbled market square and held up his hands. "Quiet! Quiet, all of you!" he shouted.

But it was difficult to bring the crowded square to order. The meeting had been moved out into the square as soon as it

became obvious that, this time, the village hall was not big enough to hold the number of people who had turned up. The news about the possibility of there being vampires in the area had spread like wildfire. And now the mayor was confronted by not only villagers, but also farmers and countryfolk from all over the surrounding district. Some of them had come on foot, some on horseback, and whole families had arrived in horse-drawn carts. And all of these, and the local villagers themselves, now stood, shoulder to shoulder, rank upon rank, filling the cobbled square and even spilling over as far as the narrow, timbered alleyways beyond. They were arguing, jostling, pushing, shoving, muttering, complaining, treading on each other's toes and generally making a nuisance of themselves.

The mayor waved his arms again. Then, realizing that he was getting nowhere, he leaned down and muttered to Alphonse Kropotel who was standing at the foot of the ancient cross. "I think you'd better see if you can talk some sense into them, Sergeant," he said. "I'm getting nowhere."

Kropotel tugged himself up on to the stone platform. His buttons gleamed in the sunlight. His boots had just had a new coat of polish. His official bearing demanded attention. He rapped with his swagger-stick on the stone cross. "Silence!" he roared. "Silence! At once! Or I'll fine every man, woman and child in this square thirty gumbeks for causing a disturbance of the peace!"

The silence was total and immediate.

There was not a movement anywhere—save for a small cloud of drifting, feathery down above the head of an old woman who was squatting on a stone stump, plucking away at a turkey carcase.

Police-Sergeant Alphonse Kropotel shaded his eyes against the glare of the morning sun and surveyed the sea of upturned, anxious faces, most of which he recognized. There was the pot-bellied, white-aproned figure of Eric Horowitz, the shop-keeper, standing in the front row with, next to him, his sharp-faced wife, Irma. Behind the Horowitz's, Kropotel could see the red-headed village washerwoman, clutching her usual bundle of dirty linen. A little way to the left of the washerwoman stood the old man, Ernst, in a cloud of pipe-smoke. While, to the right of Ernst, towered the burly, beefy, red-necked figure of Omal Hummelshraft, the dairy-farmer who, it was said, was stronger than an ox and who, to prove the point, rose before cockcrow and wrestled one-handed with his oxen every morning.

"You stupid fools!" bellowed Kropotel at the entire assemblage. "You stand here chattering and arguing amongst yourselves while your very lives may be in danger!"

The massed ranks of peasants shuffled their feet and looked down at the ground in embarrassment. There was silence in the market square broken only by the cooing of the snow-white pigeons on the red-tiled roof-tops.

The red-headed washerwoman was the first to speak. "Tell us what happened yesterday, Sergeant Kropotel?" she said, shifting her bundle of dirty linen from under one arm to the other. "Did you pay a visit to the Castle Alucard?"

"Did you see the stranger?" shouted Eric Horowitz.

"Is there any truth in the rumour that he may be a vampire?" demanded Omal Hummelshraft, the farmer, who was probably the only man present brave enough to utter the dreaded word aloud.

A shudder of horror ran through the crowded square.

Kropotel did not answer immediately. Instead, he tapped his swagger-stick into his open gloved hand for several seconds, keeping his audience on tenterhooks. Then, at last, he spoke. "Oh, yes," he said. "I went all right. Make no mistake about that, my friends. I was at the Castle Alucard. Believe me, Police-Sergeant Alphonse Kropotel knows where his duty lies — Arghh!" The police-sergeant broke off with a cry of pain as something hard and sharp dug into his ribs.

It was Henri Rumboll's elbow.

"I was there too, don't forget!" hissed the mayor. His term of office ended in a fortnight's time and he was looking for re-election. His recent act of heroism, he had decided, might just help to swing him sufficient votes. "Tell them that I accompanied you, Kropotel, or we may be looking for a new sergeant of police!"

Kropotel frowned. He had been hoping to bask in all of the glory himself but it looked as though he was going to have to share it. "Your gallant mayor, Henri Rumboll, and myself," he began again, "with no thought for our personal safety, undertook the perilous journey to the Castle Alucard, taking our lives in our hands and venturing where no man has ventured for over a score of—"

"Get on with it, Kropotel!" shouted a villager.

"Yes, come to the point!" called another.

"Stop beating about the bush!" cried a third.

"Tell us the facts, Mister Policeman!" boomed out the voice of Omal Hummelshraft above all the rest. "Is there or is there not a vampire in the district?"

Another horrified gasp went up from all around the market square at the very mention of the word.

"That is not the point at issue," said Kropotel with a careless shrug. "Would a man who was *not* a vampire travel round the area pretending to be something he was not? English? German? French? Italian? Using a different alias to every person that he comes across?"

"No!" cried a score of voices.

"And would a man who was *not* a vampire pitch his tent within the very shadow of the Castle Alucard's walls?"

"Never!" And this time the cry went up from a hundred throats.

Kropotel paused again before dropping his final bombshell. "And would the *wife* of a man who was not a vampire, and who was therefore not a vampire herself, consort with the fearsome Alucard wolf-pack—go up to them, talk to them, touch them even as if they were pet dogs?"

98

"Aaaahhh!" A gasp of horror was breathed out by every single person in the market square.

"My friends," continued Kropotel, sternly, "I greatly fear that we are plagued with not *one* vampire, but an entire family of them!" The policeman stroked at his beard to give an added emphasis to his next words. "The question is," he went on, slowly, "what are we going to do about them?"

"Destroy them!" shouted a villager.

"Kill them!" screamed a second.

"Burn them!" yelled a third.

"Besiege the Castle Alucard!" demanded yet a fourth villager.

"But they're not *in* the Castle Alucard," one of the less violent of the villagers pointed out, and added: "They've got a tent." His name was Hans Grubermeyer. He was a small man with spectacles and a straggly moustache. He was the village shoemaker.

No sooner had Grubermeyer spoken than he heard himself shouted down with boos and hisses by the vast majority of the villagers. After all, there seemed to be little to be gained from a whole host of angry peasants besieging one small camping-tent.

"They soon *will* be in the castle," argued the fourth villager, "if we don't do something about them—and quickly!"

An angry shout of agreement rose from the crowd.

"Wooden stakes, that's what they need!" It was the voice of the giant farmer, Omal Hummelshraft, that could be heard above all the rest. "Wooden stakes driven right through their evil hearts!"

Kropotel raised a hand, indicating that he wished to speak. The villagers, remembering the policeman's threat about fining each and every one of them, immediately fell silent.

"I think it's time we took a vote on it," he said. "All those in favour of besieging the Castle Alucard and destroying the vampires for all time, raise your right hands!"

Right hands shot up and waved, wildly, everywhere until the market square looked like a field of corn in a high wind.

"Hands down. All those against?"

A solitary hand went up. It belonged to the village shoemaker and it was met with jeers and catcalls. Grubermeyer blinked behind his glasses and looked around apologetically. "I'm not against destroying the vampires for all time," he said. "I just don't think there's any need to besiege the castle— particularly as there's no one in there."

"Shut up, Grubermeyer!" roared Hummelshraft, the bull-necked farmer, who then turned towards the police-sergeant. "How soon do we leave?" he demanded.

Kropotel considered the question. "I think we ought to wait until tonight," he said. "We'll attack them under cover of darkness. Take them by surprise."

"We shall need to go well armed," said Hummelshraft.

"Oh, undoubtedly," said Kropotel. "We shall need to go bearing the usual weapons: scythes, hayforks—that sort of thing—anything sharp or pointed—"

"Do you hear that, all of you?" bellowed the barrel-chested farmer at the crowd, interrupting what the police-sergeant was saying. "You must go home now and return here again at dusk, bringing your weapons with you."

"Will we need to bring goat's cheese and shrubel-cake as well?" It was the shoemaker who had voiced the question.

"Goat's cheese and shrubel-cake?" repeated the farmer,

puzzled. "Whatever for?"

"In case we're there all night," said Grubermeyer. "In case we should get hungry."

Hummelshraft turned purple with rage and his eyes looked as if they might pop out. "Goat's cheese and shrubel-cake!" he roared. "Of course you won't need goat's cheese and shrubel-cake! We're going on a vampire-exterminating expedition— not a picnic! But you'd better stick a couple of garlic bulbs inside your pockets, just in case. Right, Sergeant?"

Up on the narrow stone platform, Kropotel scowled. He didn't much care for the way in which Hummelshraft appeared to be taking things over. But there was little Kropotel could do about it. Hummelshraft was twice as big as he was and no-torious for his bad temper. Kropotel had no desire to tangle with Hummelshraft, and certainly not in public.

The police-sergeant shrugged. "It might be wise to have a garlic bulb about your persons," he advised the crowd, agreeing with the farmer.

"That's settled then," shouted Hummelshraft. "We'll meet back here at dusk with scythes and hayforks. I'll sort out a mallet and some wooden stakes. You'd all better bring along blazing torches as well! We'll give those vampires something to think about!"

The square had almost emptied as Kropotel and Rumboll stepped down from the stone platform. A pile of turkey feath-ers marked the spot where the old woman had sat.

The mayor and the police-sergeant watched, in silence, as Omal Hummelshraft swung his huge body across the broad back of the sheepskin-saddled carthorse. But, big as it was, even the massive mount sagged slightly under the farmer's bulk.

Hummelshraft clicked his tongue behind his teeth and the carthorse lumbered off, unsteadily, along the road that led out of the village, its hooves clip-clopping on the cobblestones.

"Wasn't that rather a foolish suggestion of Hummelshraft's?" said Rumboll, turning back to the police-sergeant. "Telling everyone to bring along a blazing torch? I thought the general idea was to *surprise* the vampires? Don't you think you should have contradicted him?"

Kropotel frowned and shook his head. He had no intention of admitting to the mayor that he was afraid of the short-tempered farmer. "I thought it was quite a *good* idea," he lied. "We'll need something to light our way through that pine-forest—unless you were considering climbing down that mountain again, in the dark?"

"No—no," murmured Rumboll who, to tell the truth, hadn't given the matter any thought at all.

"In which case," Kropotel continued, "the torches will be useful if we come face to face with any of those wolves. Besides, if you disagreed with Omal Hummelshraft—why leave it all to me? Why didn't you tell him so yourself?"

The mayor did not reply. He, like Kropotel, was terrified of the burly farmer but, again like Kropotel, he had no intention of admitting the fact. "I think I'll go and see if I can find my old scythe," he said. "It'll probably need sharpening up."

Mayor Rumboll walked slowly across the market square towards the narrow alleyway that led to the post office and his home, deep in thought. What was it that Kropotel had said to him? If he disagreed with Hummelshraft, why didn't he come out and say so? What right did the police-sergeant have to speak to him, the mayor, in such terms? Alphonse Kropotel, he decided, was getting far too big for his highly polished boots. As soon as the forthcoming election was over, and he had been returned as mayor, one of the first tasks he would take upon himself would be the appointment of a new sergeant of police. And about time too! Henri Rumboll nodded to himself, happily, delighted at the decision he had just reached, increased his pace and began to whistle as he walked along.

Back in the square, Kropotel's eyes never left the mayor's back as Rumboll walked up the alleyway. The police-sergeant tapped his stick against his calf. What was it the mayor had said to him? Why hadn't he contradicted Hummelshraft? What right did Henri Rumboll—a jumped-up stamp-licker—have to speak to him, the sergeant of police, in such a fashion? Rumboll certainly wouldn't get *his* vote at the forthcoming election. "Nor anybody else's neither, I should hardly think!" said Kropotel, smiling to himself. No, Henri Rumboll didn't stand a dog's chance of being elected mayor again! Well, not in Police-Sergeant Alphonse Kropotel's opinion. And a good job too! Kropotel rocked on his heels and began to hum a merry little tune. It was going to be so much easier being the sergeant of police without having Henri Rumboll sticking his long nose into everything!

Kropotel moved off across the square. It had occurred to him that he would need more than his truncheon for the task in hand. He was wondering whether he knew of anyone who might have a spare hayfork they would lend him for the night's work that lay ahead.

8

The fear-crazed rabbit broke from cover and raced across open country with the full wolf-pack in howling pursuit.

The early morning vigil kept by the wolf-pack leader and his two companions at the rabbit-warren had quickly increased in numbers. One by one, the other wolves had awakened, licked at their chops, sniffed at the pine-scented air, and then padded towards the rabbit-holes. It had not proved a successful morning. Down in the snug safety of the warren, the rabbits had easily picked up the tangy smell of wolf and not one of them had ventured so much as a twitching nose into the open air.

All morning long, the rabbit families had skulked in the comfort and safety of their holes while, outside, the wolves had padded fretfully to and fro, whining occasionally as the hunger pains gave sharper tugs than usual in their lean, starved bellies.

And then, as the morning sun climbed higher and higher in the cloud-flecked sky, a male adult rabbit, thinking more of its young ones than its personal safety, had dared to steal forth. Choosing a disused bracken-covered hole that lay some distance from the main run, the artful buck, head down, ears flat, stomach pressed hard against the ground and keeping to the cover afforded by a natural furrow, had managed to wriggle forward some twenty-five or thirty yards without being spotted. It was a useless, if heroic, endeavour. The very moment that the rabbit had dared to steal out into the open country it had put itself in full view of the ravenous wolf-pack.

The pack-leader's mate was the first to catch sight of the quarry out of the corner of one bloodshot eye. With little more than a half-choked snarl the rangy she-wolf had whipped round and, in one movement, put all of her weight on her back haunches and also aimed herself for the chase. Then, like a bolt loosed from a cross-bow, the she-wolf had flashed off in pursuit of the buck-rabbit now in full flight. The rest of the pack, needing no bidding and driven on by the gnawing in their empty bellies, had sped off hard on the she-wolf's heels.

Had the rabbit kept to a straight line across the open countryside, its chances must have been less than hopeless, for the buck could never hope to match the wolves for speed alone. But natural instinct, coupled with past experience, made the rabbit pursue a zig-zag course, forcing the wolves to change direction a score of times and, on each occasion, beating them for agility on every nimble turn.

The chase had gone on for some twenty seconds—although it seemed more like an eternity to both pursuers and pursued—when the buck-rabbit succeeded, more by luck than by design, in doubling back on its original line of flight and now found itself with the familiar territory of the rabbit-warren in its sights. This stroke of good fortune almost proved the hunted animal's undoing for, with the shelter of its home in view, the rabbit forsook its previous zig-zagging policy and made straight for the warren.

The pursuing wolf-pack, driven on now by the sudden

realization that they were in danger of losing their prey, seemed to find extra speed in desperation and quickly began to gain strides on the buck.

But the rabbit had one more piece of good fortune. Standing in a direct line between the warren and the chase was the Hollins family's encampment consisting of the battered saloon car and the pitched tent. The rabbit skimmed past the bonnet of the car, missing it by inches, and then shot clean through the tent, in at one set of open tent-flaps and out the similarly opened tent-flaps at the other end, skipping neatly over the empty sleeping-bags, folded clothing and other camping paraphernalia that it encountered on its way.

The chasing wolf-pack, following tight on the rabbit's heels and taking exactly the same route, did not have so easy a passage through the tent. Racing as they were now in close

formation, the wolves attempted to go through the open tent-flaps at one and the same time. They succeeded only in knocking down a tent-pole which then resulted in the tent collapsing about their ears, trapping them beneath its folds and leaving the entire pack tangled under the mass of canvas with their paws caught up in sleeping-bags and camping equipment. The wolves threshed and floundered and howled and whined with despair.

Across the grassy slope, Count Alucard watched, sadly, from the castle window, as the buck-rabbit scampered to safety and the wolves proceeded, in their anger and frustration, to rip the tent-canvas to shreds. "Poor things," he whispered softly to himself and then, turning apologetically to face the two visitors seated in his room, continued: "My ancestor used to call them the children of the night, you know."

"Called *who* the children of the night?" asked Albert Hollins, puzzled. As yet, he was totally unaware of the wolves' existence—let alone of the fact that they were ripping his tent to pieces.

Count Alucard shrugged. "It doesn't matter," he said with a sigh. His visitors, he had decided, had more than enough on their plates at that moment without the extra worry of knowing they would have nowhere to lay their heads that night. He turned to Henry. "Tell me everything you know about your mother's disappearance," said the count.

Henry shook his head, despairingly. "There isn't much to tell," he said. "She'd gone when we woke up this morning."

"That isn't like Emily at all," put in Albert. "I'm usually the first one up and about. She *never* gets up before I've taken her a cup of tea in bed—or in her sleeping-bag while we've been on holiday."

"We wondered," said Henry, "if she might have come up here to fetch some water from the pump, then wandered into the castle and lost her way—perhaps got locked in a room or something?"

Count Alucard's long fingers waved in the air, refuting the suggestion. "She hasn't been near here," he said. "I'd have been sure to see her. But if it would ease your minds, we can search the castle."

"If you're sure it wouldn't be putting you to any trouble, Count," said Albert.

"No trouble at all. Quite the contrary, in fact—I'd be delighted." The count tossed his red-lined cape, carelessly, over one shoulder and adjusted his black bow-tie. "Come along," he said. "Follow me—I'll lead the way."

Ushering his visitors out of the room in which he lived, Count Alucard proceeded to show them all over the ancient castle.

He led them first to the topmost, crumbling turret and, from that starting-point, they worked their way down narrow, winding, worn stone staircases through every single nook, corner and cranny to the lowest, dankest dungeon. Not many of the vast, high-ceilinged rooms they passed through were furnished, but almost all of them, in one way or another, bore witness to an age of elegant living that had long since disappeared. There was the huge ballroom, for example, with its peeling golden ceiling and its tarnished chandeliers where, once, a thousand glowing candles had flooded the room with shimmering light. There were the many exquisitely panelled bedrooms with their craftsman-carved four-poster beds, the heavy brocaded hangings of which now hung in faded tattered

shreds. There were the living-rooms, the reception rooms, the withdrawing rooms, the guest rooms, the servants' rooms. There was the darkly impressive library with its stained-glass windows and the row upon row upon row of empty book-shelves—with only the odd, discarded, mouldering leather-bound volume gathering dust on the floor to hint at the wealth of literary knowledge that had, at some time, been contained within the room.

There was also, just off the courtyard, a gigantic coach-house in which there stood the many carriages, coaches, dog-carts and other wheeled conveyances which had, in times gone by, been used to carry the castle's inhabitants when they travelled abroad, or merely took the air in the castle's grounds. There was even a large sleigh with cracked and ageing leather seats, its bodywork finely decorated with gilded curlecues and scrolls and hung with silver bells on red velvet cords. The harnessing

for all these vehicles was hung around the grimy whitewashed walls.

The coach-house was the last place they visited on their tour of the castle. Count Alucard, who had proved an excellent and most informative guide, led his two guests into the flagstoned courtyard. Henry decided that he had enjoyed the coach-house most of all, but Albert Hollins had been equally impressed with everything he had been shown.

"My word though, Count!" enthused Albert. "It's certainly been an eye-opener for me! I don't know when I last enjoyed myself so much. Why, if you could only transport this castle, lock, stock and barrel, into the English countryside, it would make a smashing stately home! You'd earn a fortune from the coach-trippers—you would—a blinking fortune! Wouldn't he, Henry?"

Henry nodded his head enthusiastically.

Count Alucard gave a little formal bow. "Thank you," he said. "It's extremely kind of you to say so. I'm delighted that you enjoyed my sight-seeing walk around—and I'm only sorry that we didn't manage to find Mrs Hollins on the way."

Albert gulped.

Henry swallowed, twice.

They had become so caught up in their exploration of the Castle Alucard that they had both quite forgotten their original reason for making the tour.

"Mum!" gasped Henry.

"Emily!" groaned Albert. He glanced at his watch and his mouth dropped open in surprise. "And just look at the time!" he said. "It's halfway through the afternoon already. Doesn't it fly when you're enjoying yourself? Emily's been missing now for over six hours! I wonder what's become of her? I do hope she's all right."

The count led the way back into the castle through the coach-house door. Albert hung back for a moment and glanced, firstly, at the darkening sky and then across and through the courtyard gates at the winding path that led down the gentle grassy slopes. But there was neither sight nor sound of Emily. Albert shook his head, frowned, and then followed Henry and Count Alucard inside, closing the coach-house door behind him.

Emily Hollins stood back, folded her arms, and admired her handiwork in the golden glow of the flickering candles she had dotted around the vaulted walls.

"There now!" she said to herself. "If nothing else, it certainly looks better than it did before!"

Emily was right. She had improved the appearance of the place. It did not, she had to admit, come up to the exacting house-proud standards that she set herself back in the cosy living-room of her home but, under the circumstances, considering she was trapped in an underground tomb, she felt she had not done a bad job at all!

After the three wolves had left the top of the hole into which Emily Hollins had tumbled, she had taken stock of her surroundings. Although she firmly believed that it would not be long before the animals returned with help, Emily could see little reason for sitting around and twiddling her thumbs. Then, as she gazed about, accustoming herself to the gloom of the chamber in which found herself, Emily's eyes had widened in surprise. She had fallen, she realized, into some sort of underground burial-place.

Inside the vaulted walls of the chamber, Emily could make out at least half a dozen stone platforms on each of which there rested a long, black, polished box with ornate brass handles attached to the sides. And, had Emily been in any doubt as to the contents of the ominous boxes, there was no need for her to remain in ignorance for long. The lid of each of the boxes was propped open and stretched out in the crimson-padded interior was a grinning skeleton!

She had, without knowing it, discovered the long-lost tomb of Count Alucard's vampire ancestors.

Emily let out a short, sharp, horrified gasp.

Not that the skeletons themselves were the cause of her misgivings. No, Emily Hollins was not the sort of woman to be scared by a few old dry bones. It was not that she saw herself as any sort of fearless heroine. Far from it. Why, there were some things that could really put the wind up Emily. A long-legged hairy spider lurking in the bath, for instance, was enough to make her shriek for Albert's assistance. A furry mouse scuttling across the kitchen floor was sufficient to send her into screaming hysterics. But a harmless skeleton, being neither creepy nor crawly, held no fears whatsoever for Emily.

And so, if it were not the skeletons that had given her cause for alarm, what was it?

Simply, the many years' accumulation of dust and dirt.

Emily Hollins was a stickler for cleanliness. The neat and new-pin appearance of the Hollins' home in Nicholas Nickleby Close, Stapleford, bore silent witness to this fact. If so much as a speck of grime ever dared to show itself on the front-room polished sideboard, it didn't stand a dog's chance. Emily, armed with duster and polish, would be attacking it in a trice.

The underground tomb, Emily saw, was inches thick in dust and dirt. She clicked her tongue in disapproval. If she herself was ever laid to rest in such unhygienic surroundings—why, she would never lie easy in her grave for so much as a second! There was only one thing for it. While waiting for the faithful guard dogs to return with help, she would pass the time by giving the tomb a bit of a spring-clean—regardless of the fact that it was not the right season.

An initial search of the darker recesses of the vaulted chamber resulted in her coming across a pile of candles in a niche in the wall. As luck would have it, she found a book of matches in her handbag and, before long, the sombre room was glowing with pools of light—certainly sufficient light to work by. Also, to her great joy, she discovered a besom broom propped up in a corner of the tomb. A large handkerchief she carried in her handbag would serve as a duster. True, she lacked any kind of cleaning-wax or polish—but Emily had discovered, years before, that good old-fashioned elbow-grease served as a useful substitute for both of these products.

Setting to work with a will, Emily toiled long and diligently and the spotlessness of the tomb now reflected her efforts. The floor-tiles gleamed. The marble shone. The dark-wood coffins glowed; their brass fitments sparkled in the candlelight. Even the silent skeletons seemed to wear a more contented smile.

And not until then, when her self-appointed task was completed, did Emily allow herself the little luxury of leaning back on one of the marble pillar supports, and taking a breather.

"Oooh, that's better!" she said to herself, relaxing in the self-satisfaction of a job well done.

But her pleasure was to prove shortlived. Glancing upwards through the hole by which she had entered, Emily was surprised to see that the sun was setting and the evening drawing in. How quickly the day had gone! It had been early morning when she'd fallen into the tomb. She must have toiled away all day, caught up in her work, unaware of the passing hours. "Doesn't time fly when you're enjoying yourself?" she said to herself.

But a disturbing thought occurred to her. If all those hours had passed since her four-footed friends had gone back to the castle, why hadn't they returned with someone long ago? Something was wrong. The guard dogs hadn't been able to make anyone understand. Help was not on its way. And what had happened to Albert and Henry? Was she going to have to spend the night inside the tomb? It was getting colder. She pulled her cardigan up around her neck and shivered slightly. All at once, she began to feel helpless, alone—and a little afraid. . .

"Come along, Emily!" she said sharply to herself. "This won't do at all! You're going to have to pull yourself together, my girl! If help isn't on its way—why then, it's up to you to help yourself!"

But how? There was no way by which she could reach up to the hole through which she had entered. There was nothing in the underground chamber that she could stand on. The only movable objects in the place were the long, black coffins and they were far too heavy for Emily to shift herself. Her thoughts pursued other directions. Was it possible that there could be another way out of the underground chamber? She had been so busy tidying up the place—and so certain in her own mind that she was going to be rescued—that she hadn't bothered to examine the tomb for any other exit.

Well then! Now was the time to begin!

Taking up one of the candles and holding it in front of her face, Emily moved along one wall, inspecting it closely. But there was no sign at all of any break in the thick-block granite sides of the chamber.

An idea occurred to her. At one end of the tomb, she remembered, there was an alcove into which she had swept the dust and rubbish. She had not paid much attention to the alcove at the time, but might it not conceal a door of some kind?

Crossing the chamber quickly, Emily held up her candle and peered inside the dark and gloomy recess. *Yes!* There *was* a door: right at the very back of the alcove and half hidden by the many years' accumulation of dust and grime.

Brushing away some long-deserted cobwebs, Emily first set down her candle and then took a firm hold on the iron door-ring with both her hands. Turning the ring, which moved with difficulty, she pushed. The door creaked open.

The narrow passage which stretched away in front of Emily was as black as pitch. There was no knowing what lay at the other end of the dark tunnel. Would it lead to freedom or might it not end in disappointment and yet another solid granite wall? There was only one way to find out.

Emily picked up her candle. The flame flickered and then steadied itself, giving off a small but comforting circle of light. She was about to set off when she remembered something she had almost forgotten. Emily stepped back into the tomb and collected what it was that she was taking with her. Then, returning to the passage and holding the candle in front of her, she set off, slowly but resolutely, into the dark.

9

"Vampires beware!
Vampires take care!
From house and farm and cottage too,
We march together stout and true.
We come to put an end to you!
Vampires take fear!
Your end is near!"

With voices raised in song, the long procession of villagers and countryfolk wound its way, snake-like, through the pine-forest. Some of them had brought along different kinds of farming implements, all of which were either sharp or pointed. As well as these weapons, many members of the procession carried blazing torches which they held high above their heads. For the evening shadows were already lengthening into night and the more nervous of the villagers cast many an anxious glance into the undergrowth for signs of the dreaded wolf-pack.

At the very head of the procession, Omal Hummelshraft, the burly farmer, looked neither to right nor left as he led his army ever onwards towards the Castle Alucard. In his right hand was a large mallet and, under his left arm, he carried a number of sharpened stakes. It was Hummelshraft's voice, louder than all the rest, that led the singing.

> *"Vampires beware!*
> *Vampires despair!*
> *From valley, hill and mountainside,*
> *From here and there and far and wide,*
> *We'll seek you out where'er you hide!*
> *Vampires take fright!*
> *Your end's in sight!"*

Marching along just behind the farmer, Police-Sergeant Alphonse Kropotel was grim-faced and silent. He had no intention of joining in with the procession and singing the old folksong.

For one thing, he was furious at the way in which Hummelshraft had taken it upon himself to lead the procession. When the villagers had first formed up in the market-place, Kropotel had put himself at the forefront of the march. They had scarcely swung out of the village and on to the mountain road, however, when he had felt himself shouldered aside by the big, beefy farmer.

Coupled with which, thought Kropotel, it was all getting too ridiculous for words! The original plan as he himself had laid it out to the villagers had been to take the vampires by surprise. Hummelshraft had spoiled all that by telling the villagers to bring torches and now—as if *that* hadn't been bad enough— here he was getting them to sing out at the tops of their voices! Take the vampires by surprise indeed! Some hopes!

Kropotel scowled, tucked his swagger-stick firmly under one arm, clutched his hayfork tightly in the other, pulled in his chin, thrust out his chest, kept his mouth clamped shut, and strode along in a smart and policeman-like manner. At least he could be a credit to his uniform. He wouldn't amble along, bellowing out, as if he was one of this loud-mouthed rabble.

In contrast to the police-sergeant, Mayor Henri Rumboll was singing as loudly as he could. It had been a good idea of Hummelshraft's, thought Rumboll, to get them all to sing as they marched along—particularly through the darkening pine-forest.

Rumboll took a tight hold on his scythe and glanced, nervously, into the undergrowth on either side. But there was neither scent nor sound of the wild-eyed ravenous wolves. It was the singing that was scaring them off, decided Rumboll: the singing and the blazing torches. The blazing torches had been Hummelshraft's idea too.

Henri Rumboll was beginning to revise his opinion of the giant farmer. Omal Hummelshraft wasn't such a bad sort after all. Not only big *and* strong, but intelligent as well! The sort of man who'd make an excellent sergeant of police.

Mayor Rumboll glanced across at Kropotel who was strutting along at his side. Kropotel had a frown on his face. His mouth was shut tight. He was striding out like a pompous peacock! Arrogant fool! Thinks he's better than the rest of us! Yes, as soon as the election was over and he was safely installed as mayor for another year, Henri Rumboll would definitely do something regarding the post of police-sergeant!

Alphonse Kropotel sneaked a glance at the mayor who was waddling along at his side. Like a fat-bellied pig! Silly old windbag! Thinks he can boss everyone around! Yes, it would be a great day when the conceited fool lost the next mayoral election. Kropotel allowed himself a little secret smile.

"Sing up, all of you!" roared Hummelshraft, turning round,

waving his mallet above his head, and urging his fellow-marchers into yet another chorus of *Vampires Beware!*

The long procession of villagers marched on, singing noisily, under the widespread branches of the tall trees, along the thick carpet of pine-needles that crunched beneath their feet, towards the grassy slope that rose up to where the dark and mysterious Castle Alucard stood in the shadow of the mountain-peak that lay silhouetted now in the moonlit sky.

"Do try a peach," said the count, pushing the fruit-bowl across the table towards his visitors. "They really are quite delicious."

Both Albert and Henry Hollins shook their heads.

Count Alucard selected one of the most succulent of the peaches for himself. He bit into it with his long, sharp teeth. The golden juice spurted out and ran down his pale slim fingers. "How about a piece of shrubel-cake then?" he suggested, proffering the appropriate plate. "It's our national dish."

Albert studied the dark brown concoction unenthusiastically. "What's it made of?" he asked.

"Sour cream, chopped almonds, ground dried figs and the whites of goose-eggs mostly."

"No, thanks."

"But you've neither of you eaten anything at all!"

"We're sorry, Count," said Henry, rising and pushing back his chair. "You'll have to forgive us—you see, we're worried about Mum."

"She's been gone all day now," said Albert, also getting to his feet. "It's most unlike her!" It was a phrase he had been repeating, on and off, for several hours now.

"I was wondering," began Henry, "whether it might be worth our while to drive into the village?"

"What for?" asked Albert.

"To see if we could organize some sort of search party."

"In the *dark*?" said Albert, doubtfully.

"They could bring blazing torches," suggested Henry.

Albert shook his head. He had a poor opinion of the villagers and held out small hope of enlisting their assistance. "You won't get much change out of that lot," he grumbled. "Most of them are barmy anyway—they go around peering at people through keyholes."

The count, who also held the villagers in small regard, nodded his head in agreement. "In any case," he said, "you wouldn't get them to come within miles of this castle once night has fallen—they go in dread of it, you know."

Henry blinked. He was gazing out of the window. "I don't think they're in dread of it at this particular moment," he said. "There's lots of them coming up here right this minute!"

Count Alucard sprang out of his chair and hurried across to the window.

The long procession was just beginning to snake out of the trees and make its way up the slope. The enormous figure of Omal Hummelshraft was plainly visible at the front, waving the mallet above his head as he exhorted his followers to sing louder than ever. Behind him, all kinds of makeshift weapons glowed in the flickering light of the blazing torches: scythes, hayforks, sickles, rakes, hoes—even the occasional boat-hook.

"Well, I never!" gasped Albert, who had joined his son at the window. "Just look at them! Just *listen* to them!" The militant sounds of the folksong were carried on the night air across the grassy slope. "They sound as if they're out for someone's blood!"

"They are," replied the count, softly and sadly. "Mine, I greatly fear."

"*Yours?*" Albert turned and gazed into the count's face, puzzled.

"I tried to tell you yesterday only you wouldn't listen," said Henry. "Alucard is Dracula spelt backwards—the count is a descendant of the real Count Dracula."

Albert's jaw dropped open. He looked the count both up and down. He took in the crimson-lined black cloak; the smooth black hair combed straight back from the high forehead; the pale complexion; the faintly red-rimmed eyes; the two pointed teeth that came down over the lower lip. . . It was as if Albert was seeing all of these things for the very first time. "You're a . . . a vampire," he said, at last. "You change into a bat at night and go round sucking people's blood!"

"No—no, I don't. I change into a fruit-eating bat. I'm a total vegetarian."

"It's true, Dad," said Henry. "Count Alucard is harmless."

"Harmless! Ha! A harmless vampire—now, that *is* a good one!" scoffed Albert. "There's no such thing."

"But it *is* true, Dad!" insisted Henry.

Albert wasn't listening. His mood was quickly changing to one of horrified anger as a terrifying thought took hold of him. "A vampire! And we pitched our tent outside a vampire's castle! We must want our heads examining! Why—it's possible that your mother's disappearance—" Albert broke off with a choking sob. The possibility was too awful to be spoken aloud—too terrible to contemplate.

"Believe me, Mr Hollins," began the count, firmly, "I know nothing whatsoever regarding the disappearance of your wife. I only wish I could help you."

Albert chewed at his lower lip, anxiously. There was something in the way the count had spoken that made Albert want to believe him. But he wasn't yet convinced. "How can I be sure of that?" he said. "And if you're as innocent as you say you are—why is it all those people out there are thirsting for your blood?"

Count Alucard held Albert's gaze, calmly and with a quiet dignity. "Because they are all fools," he said.

Albert Hollins looked deep into the count's eyes and then slowly nodded his head. The count was right. They *were* all fools. He knew that for himself. Turning his eyes away from the count's face, he glanced across at the single peach-stone on the pewter platter. "Well, I'll be blowed," he murmured. "A fruit-eating vampire-bat! Whatever next!"

Albert smiled. The count smiled. Henry's mouth broke into a wide grin.

But the moment was shortlived. The sounds of the approaching crowd were louder now and the bloodthirsty words of the folksong could be heard quite clearly through the castle window.

"What will they do to you if they find you?" asked Henry.

"Drive a wooden stake through my heart," said the count.

"But surely if you explained to them?" said Albert. "Just as you explained to me—quietly and calmly—what you really are?"

"Quietly and calmly?" repeated the count, laughing softly. "Listen to them out there! They wouldn't give me a chance to utter so much as a single word!"

"Then I'll speak to them," said Albert. "I'll go down and meet them at the castle gates and tell them exactly how things are."

Count Alucard shook his head, slowly and firmly. "They wouldn't listen to you either. They wouldn't listen to anyone—not in the mood they're in. Why, they'll drive stakes through your hearts too if they find you here with me."

"What *are* you going to do?" asked Albert.

The count shrugged. "*You're* going to leave before it's too late. I'll keep them busy in the courtyard while you make your escape."

"*No!*" said Henry fiercely. "No! You mustn't! You *can't!* They'll capture you—they'll . . ." His voice trailed away and a tear started in the corner of his eye.

"I can, you know," said the count with a sad smile. "And I must, I'm afraid. Just as you must get away—*now!*—before it's too late. Don't forget your mother's out there somewhere. Your duty is to find her."

"He's right, Henry," said Albert.

"Of course I'm right," said the count. "Quickly then! Before it's too late! Follow me!"

The count turned and strode from the room. He raced down the narrow steps that led to the lower floors, his cape flying out behind him. Albert and Henry Hollins followed close on the count's heels, their feet clattering on the worn stone, down one flight and then another.

And, all the time, they could hear the angry noise of the crowd increasing as it drew nearer and nearer the castle walls.

10

"Death to the vampires!" roared Omal Hummelshraft, brandishing the heavy wooden mallet above his head.

The crowd of villagers and countryfolk fast gathering outside the Castle Alucard took up the cry, eagerly, thrusting their own weapons and blazing torches at the night sky. "Death to the vampires!" they echoed. "Death to *all* vampires!"

"Destroy them!" yelled Eric Horowitz, the shopkeeper, waving the long sharp knife he used for cutting his cheeses.

"Drive wooden stakes through their evil hearts!" screamed the old woman, swinging above her grey head a half-plucked chicken which she was holding by one of its legs.

At the back of the crowd, Hans Grubermeyer, the little shoemaker, waved his cobbler's knife and tried to look brave as he attempted to curry favour with the crowd. "Besiege the castle!" he squeaked. "Besiege the castle!"

"Burn it!" yelled the crowd. "Burn it to the ground!"

One daredevil villager picked up a handy stone and hurled it at a stained-glass window. The glass shattered and fragments scattered all around.

The crowd cheered. But, although the courtyard gates stood open, nobody seemed over-anxious to make the first move towards actually setting foot inside the castle.

Police-Sergeant Kropotel shouldered his way to the front of the mob. Now was his chance, he reckoned, to regain his leadership from that giant clodhopper, Hummelshraft. "Friends!" he cried, holding his hayfork up in the air where its burnished prongs shone bright in the golden glow of the torches. "Fellow-countrymen!"

The crowd, waiting for someone to take the initiative, fell silent.

"If we are going to burn down the castle," continued Kropotel, "then we shall need wood—anything that will burn to start the fire going!"

"He's right!" admitted Hummelshraft. "You'll need to scour the area for kindling stuffs!" The brawny farmer swung the heavy mallet, threateningly, above his head. "The sergeant of police will keep guard with me while you're gone. We'll see that the vampires don't escape!"

Mayor Rumboll swallowed, nervously, took a tight hold on the haft of his scythe, and then stepped forward to join Hummelshraft and Kropotel. If he was hoping that the villagers would all vote for him in the forthcoming election, now was his chance to win some support. "And I, your mayor, will keep guard with them!" he announced.

"Quickly then!" bellowed Hummelshraft. "Scatter and search everywhere! Fetch sticks—logs—anything you can find!"

The crowd broke up and drifted off, in two's and three's, in search of firewood. Sergeant Kropotel, Mayor Rumboll, and the big farmer, Hummelshraft, who were standing by the courtyard gates, stamped their feet and beat their arms across their chests as protection against the chill night air.

Inside the coach-house, Count Alucard peered out through the partly open door across the empty courtyard. "Now's your chance!" he urged. "There's only three of them left guarding the gate!"

Albert Hollins looked over the count's shoulder and shook his head. "A man and a boy against three armed men?" he said. "We wouldn't stand an earthly."

"Leave it to me," whispered the count. "I'll go out into the courtyard and draw their attention—then, while they're chasing me, you'll be able to slip out through the gates."

Henry gazed up, beseechingly, into the count's dark eyes, silently pleading with him not to sacrifice himself on their behalf. But the count's mind was made up. He opened the coach-house door just a little bit wider. . .

Before he could sidle out into the courtyard though, a new development caused the count to hold back. From somewhere close at hand there came an insistent thumping noise.

Thump! . . . Thump! . . . Thump! . . . it went.

Henry, Albert and the count exchanged puzzled glances. "What is it?" asked Albert.

"I've no idea," said the count. "It seems to be coming from right under our feet."

"Do you think the villagers might have found the dungeons?" asked Henry.

The count shook his head. "There aren't any dungeons underneath the coach-house," he said. "There isn't anything under here except solid rock—" The count broke off as the thumping noise began again.

Thump! . . . Thump! . . . Thump!

They looked down at the stone-slab floor on which they were standing. It certainly looked solid enough.

"Unless. . ." said the count.

"Unless what?" said Albert.

"My father always used to say this castle was absolutely riddled with secret passages and hidden chambers. I've never bothered to look for them." He scuffed at the stone floor with his patent leather shoe. Then, reaching out, he took down a wire hand-brush that was hanging with the harness-work on the wall. Kneeling down, he rubbed, hard, at one of the slabs. "There is something set into this stone!" he said, excitedly. "An iron ring to lift it up by—it must be a sort of trap-door. Give me a hand!"

Albert and Henry got down on their knees beside the count and scraped at the rusted ring set in the stone. The three of them took a firm hold on the ring—or, to be accurate, the count and Albert took hold while Henry, from behind, put his arms around his father's waist.

"Pull!" said the count.

They pulled together. At first, the stone resisted all of their efforts. It seemed to be immovable. Then, disturbing the collected dirt of years, the slab began to shift slightly and, finally, rose up with a jolt that almost threw them off their feet.

Under the slab, a flight of dank stone steps led down to a narrow passage. Standing on the steps was a figure whose face was covered in dust, with bits of spider's cobwebs clinging to its hair.

"Emily!" gasped Albert. "What the blue blazes are you doing down there?"

"Hello, Albert! Hello, Henry!" Emily beamed through the

grime on her face as she clambered up the steps and into the coach-house. She was carrying a bundle under one arm. "Thank goodness I've found you two!" she continued. "I don't know how long I've been feeling my way along that passage—ever since that candle went out. And when I thumped on the top of those steps with my handbag—well!—I didn't know who to expect. Especially after being with those skeletons all day!"

"Skeletons?" put in the count. "Excuse me interrupting, but did you say 'skeletons'?"

Emily turned, noticing the count for the first time. She smiled, coyly, smoothed down her cardigan and patted her back hair into place. "You must be Count Alucard," she fluttered, "and here's me covered in dust and dirt!" Then, turning to Albert, she continued, sharply: "And where's your manners—aren't you going to introduce me properly?"

"There's no time now for formal introductions, Emily," explained her husband. He pointed out through the door to where, already, the villagers were returning with their arms full of firewood. "We're being besieged, dear," he said.

"Goodness me!" said Emily. "It looks as if I've jumped straight out of the frying-pan into the fire!"

"Please, dear lady," said the count, "do go on with what you were saying earlier about those skeletons!"

Emily quickly recounted the story of her underground experiences. She told them how she had fallen into the burial-chamber and how she had discovered the subterranean passage which had led her, after many twists and turns, to the spot where she had found them.

Count Alucard, who had listened keenly to every word, nodded his head. "My dear Mrs Hollins," he said, "I do believe that you have inadvertently stumbled across the long-lost tomb of the Draculas!"

"*Draculas?*" gasped Emily.

"Count Alucard is a descendant of Count Dracula," explained Henry, adding hastily: "But there's no need to worry, Mum—*he* isn't a blood-drinking vampire-bat—only a fruit-eating one."

Emily breathed a sigh of relief. "Thank goodness for small mercies!" she said.

"Thank goodness for you, too, Emily!" said Albert. "For I do believe you've arrived in the nick of time to save all our bacon!"

"How do you mean, Albert?" said Emily, preening herself at the compliment.

"Why, my love—your secret passage, of course! We can all escape along it and help each other out at the other end!"

"What a good idea, Dad!" said Henry and, turning to the count, he added: "And you can come with us too! We can *all* escape now."

"Only we'd better get our skates on," said Albert, pointing to the partly open door. Across the courtyard, the villagers were building a bonfire with the wood they had collected. "Go on, Emily," urged Albert, pointing at the trap-door. "You too, Henry—women and children first!"

But before Emily could set foot on the stone steps that led down into the passage, Count Alucard put out a hand to stop her. "Before we go, Mrs Hollins—might I ask you one question?"

"Of course you can, Count," simpered Emily. "Ask away."

"Then would you mind telling me where you found those objects you are carrying under your arm?"

Emily glanced down. In the excitement of the reunion with her husband and son, Emily had quite forgotten the things she had brought with her from the underground chamber. She held them out. "What? These?" she said. "Why, they're just some sticks I found while I was tidying up the tomb-place. I thought they'd do very nicely for tent-pegs." She turned to Albert. "You know how we're always losing them and never seem to have enough."

The count persisted with his questioning. "But whereabouts were they in the tomb, Mrs Hollins? In the coffins with the skeletons?"

Emily nodded. "That's right, Count! However did you know that? Sticking right between the bones too! They looked so uncomfortable that it didn't seem right to leave them there. I mean, how would you like someone to leave a piece of wood sticking between your bones when you're a skeleton?" The count did not reply but it was obvious from his face that something was worrying him. "Why?" continued Emily. "Did I do wrong?"

The count's long fingers toyed, restlessly, with the fastening at the neck of his cloak. "I'm afraid, dear lady, that you have removed the wooden stakes which have lain buried, all these long years, in the hearts of my ancestors."

Albert gulped. "Does that mean they'll come back to life again?" he asked.

"I greatly fear it does."

"But they were *skeletons*," insisted Emily.

"Even so," continued the count, "once the wooden stakes are removed, it is decreed that the flesh shall return—the flesh, the clothes—*and* the ability to turn into blood-drinking vampire-bats whenever night has fallen."

"It's fallen now," moaned Albert, peering out into the courtyard.

"Oh dear, oh dear," said Emily. "Whatever have I done?"

The count smiled—his slow, sad smile. "There's no need for you to distress yourself," he said. "You were not to know the consequences of your actions. But one thing is certain—you cannot venture now along that passage. Those dark alleyways may be alive with vampire-bats!"

"And it's too late now to try to sneak out through the courtyard gates," sighed Albert. "The villagers have all returned. They'll be setting fire to the castle any minute!"

Emily and the count joined Albert at the doorway.

Henry Hollins did not move. He was staring in horror at the open trap-door. "That secret passage isn't only alive with bats," he murmured, pointing towards the steps. "Look!"

Emily, Albert and the count turned from the door. They found themselves staring at the piercing eyes, slavering jaws and cruel fangs of the wolf-pack leader.

135

"Crikey!" gasped Albert, taking a backward step.

"One of the children of the night," murmured the count.

"And that's something else I've been meaning to have a word with you about, Count," said Emily. "The way you treat your guard dogs."

"G-g-g-guard dogs!" stuttered Albert. "Don't you know enough to recognize a ravenous wolf when you see one, Emily?"

As if to prove the point, the wolf-pack leader threw back its head and let out a long, loud, plaintive howl.

Ah-whoooOOOOO!

"A wolf?" said Emily, incredulously. "Don't be ridiculous, Albert—I've been feeding it tit-bits for days! Look!" And, reaching into her voluminous handbag, she drew out one of the tins of corned beef she had been carrying.

The wolf-pack leader, recognizing the tin and panting for the exquisite flavour of the food inside, crept forward up the steps and through the trap-door, wagging its tail enthusiastically and slavering with delight.

"Good boy, good lad!" said Emily, encouragingly.

The wolf-pack leader was followed through the trap-door by the first wolf which, in turn, was followed by the rangy she-wolf which, in turn, was followed, one by one, by the rest of the wolf-pack.

"Good Lord above!" groaned Albert. "There's a whole *herd* of them!"

"But they won't *hurt* you, Albert," said Emily, holding her hand out to the pack-leader. "They're as gentle as little kittens. Watch."

To the absolute astonishment of Albert, Henry and the

count, the savage beast nuzzled up against Emily and tenderly licked her fingers, one by one.

"Well, I'm dashed!" said Albert.

The arrival of the pack of wolves in the coach-house of the castle can be easily explained. Having snuffled and sniffed outside the rabbit-holes without success for most of the day, the hungry wolves had turned, accusingly, to their leader. It was up to him, they thought, to take them to food of some kind. After all, what was the point of having a leader if it didn't, occasionally and metaphorically speaking, pull the odd rabbit out of the hat? But rabbits were at a premium that day—as, in fact, was every other kind of sustenance. The pack-leader, having listened to the snarls, growls and whimpered howls of discontent, had realized that it would have to make a show, at least, of finding food for the dissatisfied pack—either that or find itself supplanted as leader by a lean, snappish, younger and stronger one-eyed wolf that had been spoiling for a fight for months. The pack-leader then, hoping to curry favour with its followers by introducing them to the curious human down the hole, had led them to the rim of the burial-chamber. Finding the human gone, and with the entire pack baying for anything to fill their empty bellies, the pack-leader had leapt down into the tomb and, followed closely by the rest of the pack, had tracked the human's scent along the secret passage as far as the trap-door and up into the coach-house.

And there the pack cringed, too hungry to do anything but ape their leader's adulation of Emily, heads cocked on one side, tongues lolling lopsidedly from their mouths, panting madly.

"Aw, bless them!" said Emily. "Aren't they sweet? Why—they'd eat out of your hand just like our rag-man's horse!"

"It's a pity they're not as big as our rag-man's horse," observed Albert, wistfully. "We could hitch a couple of them to one of these here coaches and make a dash for it!"

Henry was staring hard at the large, gaily decorated sleigh with the red-leather seats and silver bells on velvet cords. "Eskimoes have huskies to pull their sledges," he said. "Do you think it might be possible to get wolves to pull a sleigh?"

"It might," proffered Albert, gloomily. "But not unless we were blessed with some bloomin' snow!"

"Look!" said Emily, pointing up through the crack in the door at the night sky.

They looked.

A huge snowflake, sparkling in the moonlight, hung for a moment in the cold crisp air and then drifted, slowly, to the ground. It was followed by another, and then another, and then by a whole flurry of enormous snowflakes.

"We'll need to work fast," said the count, spurred into action. "Pass me down that harness-work and I'll see what can be rigged together."

Outside, by the courtyard gates, Omal Hummelshraft stamped his giant-sized boots and cursed the snow. He called out, impatiently, to a couple of late returning villagers who had yet to add their wood to the bonfire piled high against the castle wall. "Quickly!" he bellowed. "Before this weather ruins all our plans!"

Willing hands helped to toss the last dead branches up on to the bonfire. "Now!" cried Hummelshraft. "Someone hand me a torch!"

Alphonse Kropotel snatched a blazing brand from out of the hands of Horowitz, the shopkeeper. "Leave it to me," he said, moving towards the bonfire. "I'll light it."

"Just a moment, if you don't mind, Sergeant!" said Henri Rumboll, stepping out of the crowd and placing himself between the bonfire and Kropotel. "Don't you think that the lighting of this bonfire demands some sort of small official ceremony? If you'll kindly hand that torch to me, your mayor—"

Rumboll attempted to wrest the blazing torch out of Kropotel's hand, but the sergeant of police had no intention of loosing his hold. "As the principal law-enforcing officer in this district—" he began.

"Give it to me," snarled Hummelshraft, his beefy fist lifting the torch from both of their grasps. "If we wait for you two the bonfire will be buried under snow!"

Hummelshraft was right. Already there was a soft white covering of snow across the ground. The burly farmer crossed to the bonfire and touched the bottom of the pile of wood with the blazing torch. The fire caught hold immediately and a rich, red tongue of flame shot up the side of the castle accompanied by a shower of sparks. A roar of approval went up from the half-circle of watching villagers.

But Hummelshraft had barely stepped back from the bonfire when a dark shape swept down from the sky and an outstretched wing-tip brushed the side of his face. "God in heaven!" cried Hummelshraft, fearfully clutching at his cheek as the black object scudded away into the night. "Vampires! Vampires! Protect yourselves!" he cried.

The villagers stared upwards, terrified.

The vampires' skeletons, which had been returned to life when Emily withdrew the stakes from their bones, had adopted the form of blood-sucking bats and risen up through the hole in the tomb. Half a dozen, at least, of the black-winged sharp-clawed razor-toothed furry creatures could now be seen in the orange glow of the bonfire, wheeling and screaming overhead in the scurrying snowflakes.

Omal Hummelshraft struck out to right and left with his mallet and, at the same time, punched at the sky with his blazing torch. Alphonse Kropotel thrust his hayfork prongs into the air, time and time again. Henri Rumboll swung his scythe in wild strokes above his head. Eric Horowitz carved at the night with his cheese-knife. Hans Grubermeyer carried out a quick flurry of upward jabs with his cobbler's blade. The old

woman swung the dead chicken round and round, by its leg, over her grey hairs. All of the villagers and countryfolk, in fact, employing all of their improvised weapons, kept up an unceasing attack on the vampire-bats which swooped, dived, rose, re-grouped, circled again and struck about their ears.

Then, with all of this furious activity going on outside the castle walls, the coach-house doors were suddenly flung open wide in the courtyard. Four half-starved mangy wolves rushed out, yelping sharply, the pack-leader at their head, dragging behind them the antique sleigh with its silver bells jangling away on their velvet cords.

Count Alucard, whip in hand and black cloak flying out

behind him, sat in the driving seat, leaning forward, with Henry perched precariously at his side. Behind them, in the passenger seats, sat Emily and Albert Hollins, both clinging on for dear life as the sleigh rattled over the flagstones beneath the thin covering of snow. And, on either side of the sleigh, the rest of the wolf-pack bounded along, yapping and howling, their fangs gleaming in the moonlight.

Out through the courtyard gates and into the orange light of the bonfire, the sleigh raced on with the count flicking with his whip and the wolves tugging hard on the traces, picking up speed as they started to descend the slope.

Even if the villagers had *not* been fully occupied, it would have been difficult for them to halt the progress of the sleigh. As things stood, with the vampire-bats wheeling, screaming, and slashing out with tooth and claw, the desperate villagers barely noticed that the castle's inhabitants had sped through their ranks and gone.

II

Lengthening their stride, the wolves bounded on, heading now towards the familiar cover of the pine-forest. The silver sleigh-bells jingled merrily and the steel-bright runners bit into the fresh, crisp carpet of snow.

Count Alucard, tightening his grip on the reins, steered the sleigh round, gently, and aimed it towards the Hollins' camp-site. "Whoa there, my children of the night!" he called out, softly. "Whoa, now—easy—*easy* does it!"

The sleigh drew silently to a halt. The team of wolves stood panting in their traces and, as they shook themselves, a shower of snowflakes flew off their bodies in all directions.

Albert Hollins jumped down from the passenger-seat and ran towards the car, hoping against hope that the old engine would start at the first time of asking. His eyebrows shot up in surprise as he took in the ruins of the tent which had been trampled down by the wolf-pack in their earlier attempts at catching the rabbit. But there was no time now to worry about the tent or even any of their belongings which were buried under the folds of collapsed canvas. What wasn't in the car already would have to be left behind. Jerking open the car door, Albert looked back to see if his wife and son were far behind.

Emily, watched by Henry and the count, was poking about in the ruins of the tent.

"Whatever are you doing, woman?" demanded Albert in astonishment. "Come on, for heavens' sake! Move yourself! Let's get out of here!"

Emily stooped, picked up several objects and then held them aloft, triumphantly. They were tins of corned beef. "Just a minute, Albert!" she called back at her husband. "We can't go yet—not until I've fed the doggies!"

"Fed the doggies!" Albert was incensed. "You're not right in your head, Emily! If we hang around here, tossing tit-bits to ravenous wolves, we're likely to either get our blood sucked out by vampire-bats or end up with pointed stakes banged through our hearts!"

Count Alucard shook his head. "I don't think we need worry much on either of those scores," he said, and pointed across to where, in the red glow of the blazing bonfire, the villagers were swiping at the vampire-bats which were swooping around their heads. "I think they're all far too busy to bother with us!"

Emily tugged corned beef out of a tin, broke it into pieces with her hands, and tossed them into wide open, waiting, slavering jaws. "They *did* help us to escape, Albert," she said. "And it won't take long to give them a bite to eat."

"Go on then," grumbled Albert, with a little sigh. "Toss me a tin to open—I suppose the sooner we've fed the bloomin' great ugly beasts, the sooner we'll get away from here!"

Henry paused in the act of feeding the pack-leader's mate as a thought occurred to him. "What are *you* going to do, Count?" he said. "You won't be able to stay here now that the villagers know about you."

Count Alucard shrugged and shook his head. "I've *got* to stay here," he said. "I've lived here all my life, like my ancestors before me. It's the only home I know."

"It doesn't look as if you've got a home any longer, Count," said Emily.

Across the snow-covered slope, the raging bonfire had taken a fierce hold on the side of the Castle Alucard. Golden tongues of flame leapt out of an upper window. A pointed out-jutting roof trembled and then collapsed in a shower of bricks and tiles, sending smoke billowing upwards and causing a myriad sparks to shoot into the sky.

Count Alucard let out a soft cry at the sight of all this destruction.

"Why don't you come back home with us, Count?" suggested Henry.

"May I?" The count was touched at this kind offer.

Henry turned to his father. "He can, if he wants to, can't he, Father?" begged the boy.

"Well. . ." Albert paused in the act of opening a tin and wondered how his neighbours would react to the idea of having a genuine vampire living next door to them—even though it *was* only a vegetarian fruit-eating one? They hadn't been all *that* pleased, he recollected, when Henry had once brought a rabbit home for the school holidays . . . Oh, blow the neighbours! Let them think what they want! "He can come with us if he fancies it," said Albert. "What do you say, Emily?"

Emily had not been listening. She had been otherwise occupied. "Oh, look, Albert!" she cried. "I do think I've taught this one to beg at last!"

The wolf-pack leader was balanced unsteadily on its haun-

ches, its front paws sticking out in front, a sort of silly grin across its face.

"Well, I'm jiggered! Well done, Emily!" said Albert, proudly.

A short while later, when all their tins of spare food had been emptied into the wolves' mouths, the Hollins family and the count drove off through the dark silence of the pine-forest, heading for the distant coast and then home, as quickly as was possible.

The long line of cars, which stretched back along the dusty road as far as the eye could see, edged closer towards the dockside and the waiting car-ferry. Up near the head of the queue, at the wheel of the family saloon, Albert Hollins sucked at his teeth and drummed his fingers, impatiently, on the steering-wheel. Then, as the red sports-car in front of him moved forward all of a dozen feet and braked again, Albert turned and spoke, grumpily, to Henry and the count who were sitting behind him. "Would you credit it?" he said. "It's taking us as long to get on board this bloomin' ferry as it did to drive halfway across Europe!"

146

Both Henry and the count gave Albert a sympathetic smile and then, unseen by him, they exchanged a grin. Albert's observation had not been strictly true. In fact, it had been a wild exaggeration to say the least. They had not been in the car-ferry queue for more than an hour, while the journey from the Castle Alucard had taken them all of the previous night and most of that morning. But as Albert had been behind the wheel for all that time, they felt he deserved a little sympathy.

Albert sighed and shook his head. A fine sort of holiday this one had turned out to be! Vampire-bats; ravenous wolves; a village full of imbeciles who had threatened the very lives of his family and himself—and now a queue like this one! It would be a long, long while, Albert promised himself, before he allowed his wife to talk him into a holiday abroad again. It was at that precise moment he caught sight of Emily, in the seat beside him, browsing through a travel brochure of all things!

"You can put that away," snapped Albert, "as quickly as you like!"

Emily appeared not to notice the edge in her husband's voice. "There's a holiday advertised here," she said, without looking up, "that takes you on a fourteen-day coach tour through the Frankenstein country!"

"No, thanks," said Albert, through gritted teeth.

"*No?*" repeated Emily, in some surprise. "I should have thought it would have been right up your street? They take you round all the spooky castles that are mentioned in the books."

"No, thank you very much!"

In his indignation, Albert had failed to notice the two uniformed officials who, having inspected the documents of the occupants of the vehicles in front, were now moving towards

his car. One of them, a red-faced man with a pointed moustache, rapped on the car-roof with the palm of his hand while the second, who wore rimless glasses and had bushy eyebrows, bent down and peered inside the car.

Albert wound down the window.

"Excuse me, sir," said the red-faced man, "but could we see your passports?"

"Just routine, sir," beamed bushy-eyebrows. "We're from the Department of Emigration."

Albert felt in his inside-pocket, took out the family passports and handed them over. The red-faced man flicked over the pages while his companion stood, hands clasped behind his back, rocking slightly on his heels.

In the back of the car, Henry was aware of the count's long fingers fidgeting, nervously, with the hem of his cloak. It

immediately occurred to Henry what was worrying the count
—he hadn't got a passport!

"That seems to be in order, sir," said red-face, handing the
passports back. He stuck his head in at the window and peered
at the count. "And could I have a look at yours now, sir?" he
said.

"Well . . . I . . . As a matter of fact . . ." stuttered the
count. His hand fumbled for and found the car's door-handle.
He flung open the door.

The Emigration Officials exchanged an astonished glance as
Count Alucard threw himself out of the car on the opposite side
and took to his heels along the dockside.

Henry turned and stared, aghast, through the rear window.
"Come back!" he called. "Don't run—come back—it'll be all
right!"

But the count, with his long mistrust of all officialdom, was already out of earshot, running hard, as fast as his long legs would carry him, with both men in hot pursuit. The red-faced official had tugged a whistle from his shirt-pocket and was blowing short, sharp blasts on it as he ran. More men in uniform appeared from all directions around the dockside and bore down on the count.

The line of cars had again edged forward. There were several feet of space between the Hollins' car and the one in front. The driver of the car behind them, a grumpy-looking bearded man, was tooting his horn impatiently.

"All right, all right—keep your wool on!" Albert muttered to himself. He had been gazing into his rear-view mirror, watching a couple of uniformed men catch up with, and apprehend, the count. Albert sighed, released the handbrake, and the car moved forward again towards the ferry.

"Don't go yet, Dad!" pleaded Henry. "Wait for the count! We've got to help him!"

Albert shook his head. "There's nothing we can do, son. I wish there was—but they wouldn't let him come with us. Not now."

"Please, Dad! *Please!*"

"Your dad's right, Henry," said Emily. "If we don't move on we'll only get ourselves into trouble."

"But we're his *friends*! He doesn't know anyone but us!"

Emily smiled at Henry, apologetically. "It's hopeless. He's a nice man—and your dad and me are only sorry we're *not* able to help him. But if he hasn't got a passport, Henry, they'll *never* let him get on board."

The Hollins' car rumbled up the ferry's boarding runway

towards the vast black hold that waited to swallow them up. In the back seat of the car, Henry Hollins knelt up and gazed out through the rear window, biting back the tears and looking for a last glimpse of Count Alucard.

A silver moon was reflected in the gently lapping waters of the empty docks. A hundred stars twinkled in the night sky.

Inside the Emigration Building, the red-faced official walked along a white-walled corridor carrying a mug of hot sweet cocoa in one hand and swinging a truncheon in the other. He stopped outside a heavily bolted door.

"Supper-time, your highness!" he called out, jokingly, to the man within. Then, unbolting the door at top and bottom, he opened it and stepped inside. The red-faced man gulped with surprise. "Emil!" he called. "Emil! Come quick! He's vanished!"

There was the sound of scurrying footsteps along the corridor and then the red-faced man was joined by his bushy-eyebrowed companion. The two officials stood, open-mouthed, and gazed around the empty cell.

"But *where's* he vanished to, Stephan?" said bushy-eyebrows.

"Search me," said the red-faced man. "It's a mystery. The door was bolted fast on the outside. There's no other way out of here, unless. . ." He glanced up at the small barred window and then shook his head. ". . . But, no—he couldn't have got through there—nobody could."

The two officials stared at each other and scratched their heads.

Outside the small window the black bat, which had found no

difficulty in squeezing through the bars, stretched out the dry folds of its wings and gave them a preliminary flutter. Next, it walked up and down the windowsill for several seconds, getting the feel of its bat's legs, testing its sharp claws on the edge of the concrete. Finally, the bat opened its wings again, this time to their fullest extent, and then launched itself into the night. Skimming just above the water, with only the moon and stars for company, the black bat headed straight towards the empty open sea.

12

The old woman sat in her doorway with the plucked carcase of a plump goose spread across her knees. Her feet were hidden underneath a pile of goose-feathers and there were tufts of goose-down in her grey hair. Across the age-old cobbled market square, under the ancient cross, the old man sucked away, contentedly, on an empty pipe.

Several weeks had passed since the Castle Alucard had been burned to the ground. The battle with the vampire-bats had raged for hours until, eventually, the sinister creatures had been destroyed and buried again, deeper this time, and with new wooden stakes thrust through their evil hearts. It was an episode in their lives that the villagers would be happy to forget.

The old man took his pipe from his mouth, spat, and nodded at a figure that was crossing the square.

"Good morning, Mayor Hummelshraft!" said the old man.

"Good morning, Ernst!"

The mayoral election had taken place only a few days before and Omal Hummelshraft, a popular choice, was only just beginning to get used to his new title. He was on his way now to bid good morning to the sergeant of police. The appointment of

153

Hans Grubermeyer, the little shoemaker, as the new police-sergeant had come as a shock to many of the villagers. But it had been Hummelshraft's idea and it suited him well enough. Grubermeyer was not an ambitious man and was happy enough to stay out of the limelight and plod along in any direction that suited Hummelshraft who, for his part, looked forward to a quiet and enjoyable term of office.

Henri Rumboll, now that he was free from all civic duties, had more time to devote to his job as village postmaster. The backlog of work in the post office, which had accumulated while he had been mayor, was gradually being cleared. Letters and parcels that had lain around the post office for months were gradually being delivered to their rightful owners. Not that Henri Rumboll could take much of the credit for this—for most of it was due to the man who was now crossing the square in his smart new uniform.

"Good morning, Postman Kropotel!" said the old woman, tenderly stroking the pink skin of the plump plucked goose.

"Good morning, Elsa," replied the new postman.

Alphonse Kropotel shifted his sackful of letters from one shoulder to the other and strode on. He glanced down, approvingly, at the glistening toe-caps on his new boots. There were worse things than being a village postman, he had decided. The uniform was just as smart as the one he had worn as police-sergeant. Smarter, possibly! There were certainly more buttons for him to polish. The hours were not bad too. The pay was more than adequate. Of course, he still had that pompous old fool, Rumboll, to contend with—but that wouldn't last for ever. Rumboll, before too long, because of his own incompetence, would surely find himself out of a job. And then—

who could tell?—perhaps he, Alphonse Kropotel, might find himself elevated to the office of village postmaster! Kropotel whistled a merry tune between his teeth as he continued on his way.

A horse and cart, the driver asleep at the reins, clip-clopped into the quiet of the square.

A black cat preened itself in the sun and then padded off into the shadows of the alleyways.

A pair of snow-white pigeons billed and cooed on a red-tiled roof.

Life in the village was gradually returning to normal.

Epilogue

Since flying across the sea and arriving in England, Count Alucard has never once returned to human form. He has spent all of his time, in the guise of a bat, searching for his young friend, Henry Hollins. The count is never in the same place twice and he is always on the move.

Sometimes he pauses long enough to snatch a meal in a fruit-filled orchard or from a hedgerow heavy with berries. But he is soon on his way again, flitting restlessly across the tops of trees or twisting over rooftops turning in and out of chimney-pots. It is a hard task that he has set himself but one day his diligence may be rewarded.

Try hard enough and—who knows?—you might catch a glimpse of the count yourself. But if you look for him in daylight you will never see him. For, when the sun is up, the count is always fast asleep: hanging upside down in some tall church-steeple perhaps or, maybe, in a steadily ticking clock-tower or, even, in the ghostly ivy-covered shell of an ancient ruined castle.

Go out though, into street or field or garden after dark, stand staring upwards and—who knows?—you just could be lucky enough to spot Count Alucard, the very last of the vampires, scudding across the night sky. . .

Ghosts and Shadows

DOROTHY EDWARDS

Who was the lanky, bright-eyed man who haunted the football field? Why couldn't the Council Surveyor cure the misty patch of damp by the tower block lift? What had happened long ago in the old gold-prospecting town?

There are tales of today, and tales of that other world which curls closely round our own: a world of changelings, church grims and shadow-stealers, where the souls of dead seamen cry through the gulls' screaming, where a phantom horse comes galloping through the dark and demons ride the cold air of Twelfth Night.

With stories written by favourite authors especially for this book, with descriptions of strange encounters, with poems and folk-tales, Dorothy Edwards evokes the shadowy world of ghosts.

Out of the Blue

An Anthology of Weather Poems

Fiona Waters, a children's bookseller for fourteen years, has compiled this vivacious new collection of poems about the weather. Fiona's view is that poetry should be approached carefully and seriously, with respect and interest, never half-heartedly, never ponderously — and most of all it must be enjoyed.

Readers will find plenty to amuse and stimulate them in the works of traditional poets such as Walter de la Mare, John Clare, Thomas Hardy and modern-day poets including Ted Hughes, Russell Hoban and Laurie Lee. And their range of moods and styles are imaginatively illustrated by Veroni's lovely drawings.